In a world where few people side against producing children, Jim Crawford has done it for them, and done it well. The title of his book is *Confessions of an Antinatalist*, but it could just as well be *Memoirs of a Humanist*, for what could be more human than outrage at human suffering. Honesty, intelligence, and the courage to entertain us with the foibles of his own life are the prime markers of Crawford's book. Even if one loathes the idea of antinatalism on its face, the questions that Crawford raises are such that everyone would be well advised to confront, for someday they may be called upon by their offspring to answer them. And *Confessions of an Antinatalist* dares them to come up with answers they can stand by in good conscience.

>Thomas Ligotti,
>author of *The Conspiracy against the Human Race*

Confessions
of an
Anti-Natalist

Jim Crawford

ED Books

Confessions of an Antinatalist

Published by
Nine-Banded Books
PO Box 1862
Charleston, WV 25327
ninebandedbooks.com

Copyright © 2010, 2014 Jim Crawford

ISBN 10: 0989697266
ISBN 13: 978-0989697262

Editorial Assistance
Ann Sterzinger

Cover design by Joseph Clagg

To my daughters, Michelle and Sondra. Your joys are my joy, your sorrows my regret.

Prologue

Imagine you're standing at the top of a sheer, high mountain. You peer over the edge. You can't quite see the ground below, because there's a layer of fog, or clouds. But you know you're high enough that, if you jumped off, the impact would be fatal. Imagine, now, that you have a child with you—let's say, a little girl.

The thought suddenly enters your mind that it might be fun for your child to take a little flight down the side of the cliff-face. You've always dreamed about what it must be like to fly! Whatever the risks, it must be more fun than sitting around in this empty place on top of the mountain. Why, all your daughter has done since she's been here is sleep! Peacefully, to be sure, but so peacefully it's as if she doesn't even exist! But why should she not exist, when she could be FLYING? There's just something wrong with that idea.

And so you slap her on the rump to wake her up. She starts to cry, but you cradle her in your arms, and coo at her, and tell her how much you love her. You tell her how lucky she is to be alive. Your soothing voice settles her, and she hugs you as you walk back to the cliff's edge. With one last kiss for luck, you pry her arms from around your neck, and launch her over the edge—granting her the gift of flight! You watch as her form slowly disappears into the fog below.

But the fog has lifted a bit now, and you can make out some shadows that resemble boulders jutting from the cliff's face. Surely your child won't be so unfortunate as to encounter any of those. No! After all, she's your *child, and you love her so dearly. Still, you shout words of encouragement, last minute instructions and advice. At times, you catch a glimpse of her through little holes in the cloud cover. Look at her! How fast and true she soars! How proud you are of her—and of yourself, of course, for you have bestowed this precious gift to such a special child! You are a giver!*

You are so preoccupied with your child's progress that only after a time do you notice other givers gathered along the cliff's edge, casting their own children over. You become friends with some of them. You chat with one another about the marvels of giving flight, and about how good it is to see the children soar. The experience is so fulfilling, so spiritual, and you've all learned so much about yourselves, and about life.

Then a lone voice calls everyone over to the edge. His tone is one of concern, and...regret? You and the others move toward him. At once, you notice that the fog has now completely burned away. Spread out below, there is a giant, empty valley, the terrain of which appears to be much like the top of the mountain—the children's point of departure. Only the valley below is a blotchy red color. Looking closer, you see that the boulders and outcroppings along the face of the mountain, which are far more numerous than you had perceived before, are also stained with red, and seem to be blotted with little shreds of hair and clothing.

The flight-giver who was the first to notice all this begins to cry. Soon, some of the others join him. You begin to feel sad, and maybe a little guilty. But you don't really like to be sad, do you?

Another giver who doesn't want you to be sad lays her hand on your shoulder. "But wasn't it all worth it?" she asks softly, "They flew!" And she's smiling as if she almost believes what she says. You smile back. Together, you chide the few who can't smile for being pessimists. You join the welcoming committee to greet the long queue of hopeful givers bearing sleeping children in their arms, waiting for the moment when their kids, too, can fly. You counsel the new arrivals to shun the ones who weep, and you encourage them to give as you have given. In their company, you soon forget all about the strange lone voice. And you feel better. Don't you?

Well, don't you?

In The Jaws of Ouroboros

Ouroboros, that hungry snake,
found nought of what he might partake.
In desperate straits, his tail he curled,
then ate himself and shat the world.

It's an idyllic post-summer morning in the Southern California desert, though I'm not sure Riverside can properly be called that anymore. Not since around the turn of the previous century, anyway, when John Henry Reed convinced the Riverside Chamber of Commerce to greenify the place. During his seven year stint as 'Tree Warden,' approximately 15,000 trees were planted, and the tradition continued from there—in Riverside, as well as in several surrounding communities. So much the better. Endless plains of dirt and sand, occasionally interrupted by hillocks of rock, dirt, and sand, are highly over-rated in my book.

Still, in the big picture we're just a tiny oasis in the middle of 25,000 square miles of officially designated desert. And it's the middle of October. Already the Santa Ana winds have begun to do their damage—hot inland siroccos taking advantage of the flat terrain, whipping up to gusts of over 50 mph at times, relocating carelessly discarded butts and flames from hobo campfires into brush and grasses that haven't seen rain since early spring. Fires are already popping up here and there. They've been fighting one near Ventura for almost a week already. Homes will be lost; maybe a few human lives as well. And, of course, it goes without saying that the body count of dead wildlife will swell just as far as one has the inclination to count down the evolutionary chain.

But I haven't smelled any smoke yet. No cindery cloud cover hastening in the dusk before 11 AM, like that Saturday back in 2003. No lives or property threatened of anyone I know; or, more important, anybody I care about. Hopefully the worst will pass me by, and the only fretting I do will be to the images on television. I might be induced to a bit of hand-wringing, until I get tired of watching and flick the channel over to a *Seinfeld* rerun. Or go eat a sandwich. Life goes on, as they say.

They do say that, don't they? They also say, "Life is good."

I disagree.

I am an *antinatalist*. As far as philosophies go, mine is pretty cut-and-dry. I simply believe that human beings should stop breeding and let the race die out through attrition. That's not quite all of it, but it's the gist. No, I'm not formulating plans for mass extermination, nor am I pounding the pulpit for national sterilization programs. I'm just asking people to forego procreation, and providing them with ideas and information as to why this is a good choice. Why, then, is my message so universally dismissed, defied, ridiculed, and otherwise met with varying degrees of distress and hostility?

I can almost hear the chuckles of the reader who's disinclined to seriously consider my proposition, shaking his head as he regards my preposterous entreaty. I take it in stride, but I believe there are substantive answers to my rhetorical question—answers which tend to get glossed over, twisted, or not-so-subtly rationalized out of consideration. Of greater importance (and this is the ember fueling that fleck of hope sustaining my writing aspirations), is my belief that antinatalism is the logical extension of normative human sensibilities. At least, the ones most civilized people maintain as personal moral ideals. I've always been a firm believer that good arguments start from common ground. Keeping that in mind, I proceed upon the assumption that most of my readership possess some degree of empathy for their fellow human beings. Empathy encompasses such traits as compassion, interpersonal insight, and a shared awareness of the joy, hardship, longing, and suffering that are the lot of all humankind. Empathy proceeds after an understanding of the inherent inequality in the way Fate deals the cards. I can't overstate this last point, and I will return to it frequently.

Hope is my enemy. She is a succubus who descends upon sleeping humankind, whispering that there *is* a future. A bright future, as a matter of fact; as long as we persevere in extending our essences through the lives of our children, and through their children. She is a liar, a snakeoil salesman bartering chimera for generative fluid, which she sucks out of us before casting our withered husks onto the fire. And so we fall, row upon row like seasons of corn, but not until we relinquish our seed into her exploitive hands. For in the end, we all die, and only Hope lives on. And we rot, sometimes mourned for a season, but presently forgotten. Ultimately, like it or not, we are the future's dirt. This is the state of affairs we choose to subject our children to.

This is the reality I chose to bring MY children into.

DID YOU EVER have a recurring fantasy when you were a kid? One that persisted more or less intact through the various developmental thresholds encountered and crossed in the process of growing up? Maybe even carried over into adulthood?

I did.

A plague has swept the planet, the result of a government biological weapons experiment gone awry. The human race has gone extinct, replaced by the re-animated bodies of the undead. And yet, somehow, I—me, Jim Crawford, who, for some unknown reason, am immune to the supergerm released upon an unprepared and unsuspecting world— have survived. Oh! And that girl from French class who has big tits for a 14-year-old. Yeah. She's immune, too. Together we walk the earth, armed to the teeth. We seek shelter wherever we can find it, keeping just one step ahead of the zombies who resent our life force, and our love. And we fuck like rabbits, especially after a narrow escape.

Though I don't remember for sure, I suspect this particular flight of fancy was inspired by the film *The Last Man on Earth* with Vincent Price, later to be re-done as *The Omega Man*, and most recently as *I Am Legend*. Richard Matheson must be swimming in royalties. I make no claim to originality.

But the 'End of the World'—that phrase being commonly understood as the end of humankind—is never far from the collective imagination, is it? The storyboard may be revised to suit a culture, so the post-nuke aftermath becomes a zombie holocaust or, in contemporary fashion, an ecological catastrophe.

But the apocalyptic theme holds constant. It grips us. It feeds the fears and fantasies of childhood, and adulthood. The most conspicuous examples may be found in popular science fiction and horror, but the roots are purchased in deeper soil.

Consider the Bible. As a former thumper, I can assure you that nothing galvanizes the Wednesday evening prayer meeting like a trip through the Book of the Revelation. It's got everything—divine threats, locusts, blood raining from the sky, catastrophic meteor impacts, torture, eyeballs boiling, skin exploding...the fucking works! I'm telling you, that John of Patmos was the Stephen King of his time. And people eat the shit up! There's nothing more spiritually uplifting than gathering together with a few close friends, and praying for Hell to rain down on God's ugly stepchildren, the ones who didn't pass muster. Pass the wine, and hold the wafers!

What *is* this fascination? Why are we driven to contemplate, if only in a make-believe way, the demise of human existence? Settling aside the nerdling-boy-meets-otherwise-unattainable-girl-so-they-can-repopulate-the-world angle (which pretty much speaks for itself), why are we thus preoccupied?

To be entirely truthful, the answer probably consists of several facets. Alienation. Mortality salience. Oblivion as an escape route for stillborn dreams. The aspiration to light a fire under our own ennui. Etcetera.

But I'm not looking to deconstruct humanity's entire psychological gestalt here. Keeping things simple, I think the plain answer is pretty obvious, *id est*:

LIFE SUCKS.

I think I read this on a T-shirt.

ONE OF MY EARLY recollections, perhaps the earliest, is of me hiding underneath the dining room table. I believe I was around two years old at the time. If memory serves, I was ostensibly playing with a windup toy duck. But mostly, I was watching. Back and forth, disembodied pairs of legs vied for a two-year-old's attention. Thinking back, it occurs to me that most of a young child's life exists bereft of context. Things pop in and out of reality like dream images. I imagine my parents were having some kind of get-together, but all I can remember are the legs, accompanied by the background noise of incomprehensible conversation that's always present when adults commingle. There was no question of discovering any underlying meaning to the sound, or the movement; nor of discerning anything like motivation, or even direction. I felt like I was underwater, passively observing the languid swaying of seaweed in the current. Only the world wasn't 'out there.' It was more like a movie playing on the backs of my eyeballs, appearing spontaneously and sourceless, frame by frame in the ethereal mindscape that contained my self, and everything else.

My emotional states, too, were punctuated by this sense of automatic emergence into awareness. Joy, anger, melancholy (my mother tells me I was a brooding boy)—these tempers seemed to arrive divorced from any source, with no tether of justification. Or so it felt at the time. I wonder: is this spontaneous materialization of moment-to-moment personhood what some might deem to be the essence of Rousseau's noble savage? And are we hearkening back to that very early mindset when we speak of things like 'blind faith,' or 'childlike' innocence? What else could account for a grown man writing something like "Now, faith is the substance of things hoped for, the evidence of things not seen" (Hebrews 11:1, KJV)? Or, as I am prone to paraphrase this verse, "I WANT it to be, therefore it IS."

As my long-term memory developed, I soon learned there was a real world 'out there' independent of my immediate concerns—that it really wasn't all about *me* after all. Of course, the insight never arrives pre-packaged or fully formed. Internalization of such a concept develops in fits and starts, and our recognition remains blurred at the edges. From the cozy womb of preliterate solipsism, we stumble into the sensory order, confused.

At one time or another I suppose we all get drawn into the argument over whether *true* altruism exists. Well, I'm not so innocent as to believe in unadulterated selflessness. But neither am I so cynical as to suspect every motivation behind apparently genuine munificence.

Here's the way I see it. In the beginning, all of us are like tightly wound balls of string (I'm speaking of *consciousness* here; or maybe *awareness* is a better word, with the emphasis on 'self' awareness). In the physical sense, we're just as much a part of the larger environment surrounding us as we'll ever be. But our perceptive pointers are all turned inward, and *everything* is about *us*. Actually, everything IS us! The summer sun *is* the heat of our skin. The bottle of milk *is* the feeling of a full stomach; and so on.

Time proceeds. Slowly the little ball of string, jostled and batted about by the ever-changing flux of circumstance, begins to unravel. Tendrils of perception wander outwards, reconnoitering and telegraphing their discoveries back down the threads via diverse sensory pathways, altering the patterns at the core. Evoking responses. Years go by, and eventually our psychic 'selves' become more or less tangled up in the larger world. But a subtle shift has occurred. Where once the whole world existed in a ball of string, now the ball of string has become the whole world! This entanglement, especially as it pertains to other lives, is my metaphoric description of what has otherwise come to be understood as empathy or compassion. Or even pity, if you prefer.

I should emphasize that what I've described here are the polar extremes of a situation. Ultimately, all of us are both ball *and* entanglement. Selfishness *and* selflessness. Desire *and* generosity. Lust *and* abandon. The degree to which we are one or the other (an imprecise dichotomy, I'll grant, as we are always *both*), is determined by the initial state of the ball of string, as well as by the subsequent impact of the greater environment upon it. Put another way, the limits to which we psychologically extend ourselves to include others mark the parameters of our empathic selves, the capacity of which varies from person to person. I suspect this process continues somewhat farther down the food chain of the lesser sentient creation, though perhaps it's not so easily recognizable.

We care, or we don't care. We put out feelers and move forward, or we draw back. And there is conflict. Between ourselves. Within ourselves. Yet somehow, out of this morass of fallible and vacillating emotional states, there has emerged what I like to think of as a universal humanistic sensibility. An internalized set of values spanning time and cultural boundaries. A substratum of shared feeling informing our laws and customs, and lifting us above the clockwork of mechanical utilitarianism. Some may choose to label this phenomenon a 'moral compass,' though the term 'morality' is fraught with so much dogmatic baggage that I'm loath to employ it. Be that as it may, it all comes down to what we think, or perhaps more to the point, what we *feel*, about what's right as opposed to what's wrong.

Concerning that last bit, I tend to believe we're a lot closer to each other than we often let on.

I also hope to demonstrate that most of us, each deep in his/her heart of hearts, knows that bringing new life into the world is wrong. So very wrong.

On the way to school this morning, my daughter informed me that her mother's pastor has been replaced. Seems he had a crisis of faith, and began dallying in internet porn.

I wonder—did the crisis come before, or after?

Halfway through my bicycle commute today, I was forced to detour around a throng of very young Hispanic women pushing baby strollers down the middle of the sidewalk. Actually it's a daily occurrence in my neighborhood. I found myself wondering if any of them ever considered the relatively high statistical probability that their sons might grow up to be violent gang members, or that their daughters could conceivably make them grandmothers before they're out of their mid-thirties. Probably not. Adolescent motherhood, while openly scorned for its carnal implications, is common and grudgingly accepted within that particular community. And why not? Jesus loves the little chilluns of the world, *si?*

I'm not deliberately race-baiting here, though neither am I a cultural relativist. The 'old enough to bleed, old enough to breed' mindset of the Third World is quickly spilling over into the First—a resurgence of primitive attitudes I am not thrilled to witness. Whatever happened to that 'zero population growth' rhetoric popularized by the likes of Paul Ehrlich in the 1960's? Overwhelmed by the rewards of cheap imported labor, I suspect.

Despite the slight deviation from my route, I nevertheless made it to work with about 15 minutes to spare. I'm a cook in a fast-food Mexican restaurant. Since I had some time to kill before clocking in, I went ahead and slapped a breakfast burrito together, grabbed a Coke, then sat down in the dining room to choke it down. As I ate, I stared out through a window at the section of the parking lot adjacent to my side of the building, the part that feeds off the main street running parallel to the front of the store.

I had about two bites left when I saw him—the dog that's made semi-frequent appearances for at least the last two-and-a-half years I've been working there. He's a little guy. Appears to be some sort of terrier mix, with maybe some chihuahua stirred in from somewhere. Your typical Heinz 57 mongrel. He always comes in from the east side, street-smart enough to stay on the sidewalk and avoid the heavy traffic on Van Buren. I've seen him disappear through the wrought iron fence of the mini-storage place next door. Whether he lives there, or is just a stray working the handouts circuit, is unbeknownst to me.

I still had a few minutes, so I watched him, observing his body language. I lay absolutely no claim to the avocation of canine psychoanalyst, but it was easy to see that this little fellow embodied an almost perpetual state of scared shitlessness. What do you call a flinch that never quite goes away? Back hunched. Eyes darting in every direction incessantly. At one point he started running in circles, as if chasing his own tail. Only in his case, I think he was in a feedback loop of continuously trying to look over his own shoulder.

Hesitantly and erratically, he made his way up the drive—his likely destination the dumpster set at the entrance to the lot proper. I stood up and went to the doorway a couple of steps behind my seat, the stub of my burrito in my hand. Slowly, I pushed open the glass door, easing my way around the corner and into his line of sight. His startled bark reminded me more of a scream, and if his tail had been between his legs before...well, now it was grafted to his quivering belly. I knew better than to approach the poor creature. Instead I tossed the morsel in his general direction, then immediately backed up, retreating into the restaurant to watch him through the window.

After a few seconds of tremulous indecision, he lurched forward and grabbed my leavings. But instead of wolfing it down then and there, which would have only taken a matter of seconds, he held it in his jaws and hightailed it back down the drive, up the sidewalk, and was quickly out of sight.

I like to think he has a little cubby somewhere. Maybe a dug-out shallow beneath some green ferns—shady, cool, and private—where he can enjoy his little snacks in whatever passes for tranquility for him. That Bluth cartoon says all dogs go to heaven. I wish it were so.

Looking Out Schopenhauer's Window

Passions coagulate to form a man;
ancient things, born of the first wave.
Rationality the unexpected offspring,
allowed to build its Tinkertoy edifice—
that idiot savant.
"I am my own master" it boasts,

but almost never sees it coming—
the back of the hand.
Doesn't think to duck;
except, perhaps, in retrospect.

It was never different, you know?
Never a golden age.
Never better times.
Never enough wisdom.
Just pretense, born of shame—
survivalist posturing,
like a dog that bows its head to protect its own throat...
We are ravenous.

Deceit,
nested within lust,
nested within blind impulse—
the fundamental beast of existence.

Blind.
Unaware.
Unstoppable.

WE are its apologists.
We dress it up in silken robes,
and parade it before the gathered crowds.
We offer our skins in service to its charade,
placing blinders over our eyes,
lest they become portals into our own
malignancy.
To do otherwise would be to invite
madness.

Having once and for all descried
the leprous hand of the puppeteer,
the natural question might be:
Why?
But, I ask you…
who will hear the answer?

I ALWAYS FELT an affinity for Arthur Schopenhauer, even before I became familiar with his writings during my relatively brief love affair with Western philosophy. If memory serves, my initial introduction to his work came via some offhand mention by the mythologist Joseph Campbell in that great series of interviews with Bill Moyers in the 1980s. Later on, I tried working through *The World as Will and Representation*, but found myself disappointed in what I saw as just another pedantic workup of speculative metaphysics.

I eventually lost interest in all the post-ancient Greek philosophers, including the existentialists. I settled on a diet of Westernized Eastern pop-philosophy, as epitomized by the late Alan Watts (god love the old sot).

Yet Schopenhauer's pessimism struck a terrible chord. It's pretty much all the guy's remembered for these days, I suppose—this idea that there is something fundamentally and eternally negative that runs through the very fabric of existence. But for me, the idea was startling.

Because I knew it was true.

I think I had always known, as though the knowledge had been lurking right there below the surface, tucked away beneath the brittle layers of unjustified hopes and regurgitated life affirmations that keep the human hot rod forever burning rubber in this race to nowhere.

"He who lives to see two or three generations," Schopenhauer observed, "is like a man who sits some time in the conjurer's booth at a fair, and witnesses the performance twice or thrice in succession. The tricks were meant to be seen only once; and when they are no longer a novelty and cease to deceive, their effect is gone."

LIFE IS GOOD.

Life is a gift.

Life is precious.

Life is sacred.

Life is a many-splendored thing.

Let's contrast these lofty maxims against some less attractive aspects of the reality most of us are familiar with. How's about pediatric brain cancer? Chemical warfare? Incestuous rape? Crippling depression? Starvation? AIDS? Plague? Massive extermination by storm, flood, earthquake, and volcano? Genocide? Fratricide? Assassination by cyanide?

Oops, I'm rhyming. But you get the picture.

Of course, someone might be tempted to contest my logic here, perhaps with an argument like: "Look! All that stuff you've listed is real, but it's only a PART of what life's about. You've purposely left out all the good things that ultimately make life worth the price of admission."

To which I would counter with an example.

Let's take Adolf Hitler, the poster child for creepy megalomaniacs who want to rule the world. But, hey! The guy was also an artist! As a matter of fact, seeing that he couldn't make it into the Viennese art academy, he might even rightly be considered a tortured artist. Surely this is a sign that there was some higher sensibility latent in that proud Teutonic heart. I also understand he liked dogs. Now, in my opinion, no dog lover can be all bad. I'm sure the guy possessed other positive human attributes, as well. Only propagandists and dullards rest their judgment solely on caricature.

Well, then? Hitler—good guy, or bad guy? Straight from the gut. Quickly, spit it out! Okay, I'll say it for you. BAD GUY! (Goose-stepping misanthropes and Deep South trick-or-treaters, having discovered between the covers of this book neither blueprints for pipebombs fashioned of tampon casings and cowshit, nor naked pictures of their cousins, will probably have laid it down before now, so I'll assume I'm in the clear).

Was that so hard?

Now ask yourself: what's the quality of determination tipping the scales against the man with the little mustache? I offer you the answer in a nutshell. Adolf Hitler, in spite of possessing some of the personality traits most folks would deem attractive or otherwise acceptable, was also responsible, directly or indirectly, for massive amounts of human suffering and death. He was, for lack of a better word, a human monstrosity in moral terms. Probably not the worst who's ever lived, but close enough to pin the tail on. End of story—and not because my argument is the conclusion to a logical syllogism, but because I share with most of my fellow human beings a deeply felt abhorrence toward the existence of needless suffering and death, and the infliction of the same.

Suffering is wrong. Not because God says it's wrong. Not because it's the incorrect extrapolation of an extended formula involving modal logic. Not because of Platonic ideals, or Kantian imperatives, or because it produces foundational rifts in the underlying universal harmony. Suffering is wrong because *we don't like it*. It *offends* us. We don't *want* to suffer, nor do we *want* those we care about to suffer. That's why there is no suffering in Heaven (although I understand there is also no beer, so count me out).

Did I say we don't want our loved ones to suffer? Indeed, I did. Yet we continue to deliver into this existence, by means of procreation, generation after generation of children. Children whom we love, but also children who, by the very nature of things, are all condemned to suffer, and to die. In fact, a birth certificate and a certificate of death might as well be written on the same piece of paper. Death, including all the suffering leading up to it, is as inextricably bound up in the fabric of life as is the moth's attraction to the flame. Each of us is the thinnest of bookmarks, caught between the leaves of birth and death in the tome of eternal nothingness. Why, then, do we continue to feed the ever-burning fire that consumes without a trace?

Why? That's a good question. Why, indeed?

If children were brought into the world by an act of pure reason alone, would the human race continue to exist? Would not a man rather have so much sympathy with the coming generation as to spare it the burden of existence? Or at any rate not take it upon himself to impose that burden upon it in cold blood.

—Arthur Schopenhauer

I BECAME A CHRISTIAN in 1975, just a week or so before my twentieth birthday. It happened like this.

I was working at a small factory in Westminster, California. We manufactured fiberglass holding tanks for caustic liquids. My job was basic maintenance and custodial work. I unloaded trucks, moved things around with the forklift, and did most of the shitwork that gets handed down to the lowest man on the totem pole. Most of my coworkers were illegal aliens with little or no English, but there were a few white guys around—including the kid who'd gotten me the job. His dad was half-owner of the company.

I was fairly heavy into drugs in those days. Not heroin or anything like that. Just the usual white punk suburban stuff we all took for granted. A little coke now and then when we could afford it. You could still score barbiturates back then, and sheets of really good acid popped up with almost clockwork regularity. Fifty cents for a tab. There was a powdered substance—sometimes brown, sometimes white—called *kanebanol*, which nobody I've subsequently met has ever heard of. I find only scant reference to it on Google. Maybe I'm spelling it wrong. But man, did that stuff kick ass, albeit in a mellow sort of way. There was also hashish of various strengths and colors.

And there was pot. Tons and tons of it. Everybody had it. Everybody smoked it. And oddly, almost everybody shared it. 'Don't bogart that joint'—a phrase straight out of the Sinsemilla

Lexicon. As though the stuff were meant to be passed around, which was fine by me.

That was then. The folks who manufactured your toys, who operated all that heavy equipment—we were baking on the big bad boo. Doesn't it give you the fuzzies?

I remember a time when my sources had temporarily dried up and I was feeling close to desperate. My friend Tim told me there'd be shit at a party that evening. I was never much for parties, but I went along.

We were the first to arrive. I shyly snagged a beer from the kitchen, then planted myself in the corner of a couch in the darkest area of the living room, attempting to keep a low profile. The hosts were older guys in their mid-twenties. Unlike the punk-ass idiots I usually met at these things, they actually paid their own rent and didn't live with their divorced mothers. Things didn't start off well. Within two minutes, Tim, who was a bit of a loose cannon, was in a heated argument with one of the hosts. Something about a bad debt, I gathered. Soon, it became clear that Tim wasn't even invited, which of course meant that neither was I. Fucking great.

Fortunately for Tim and me, the prospect of hostility turning to actual violence was short-circuited by the arrival of other guests. The first guy came in carrying a cumbersome black case. He unpacked it to unveil a portable Fender Rhodes with sound system, and then there was music—the most incredible jazz! More people trickled in. There was a guy with an acoustic guitar, accompanied by a beautiful young blond who grabbed a stool and started singing and wasn't bad. Soon all the available seating was full, as well as a lot of the standing room, with the overflow sort of pushed into the kitchen. It seemed everybody came with booze, and I put away my share. Later on, the guy sitting next to me pulled a harp out of his pocket and started wailing with the other musicians.

I'm not sure how much time went by, but at some point Tim came up behind me and said, "Dope's here." I got up and followed him into the kitchen where a group of about twenty guests had gathered in the shape of that oh-so-familiar circle that told me these were MY PEOPLE. I jostled into position for the hand-off. There were at least four joints already making the rounds, while our itinerant provider had at least two ounces of the green spread out on the counter-top and was rolling more.

The music transformed into waves, approaching and receding, approaching and receding. I listened to incoherent bursts of conversation and laughter and I grinned like an absolute moron. I was home.

Later on, our pusher, who might as well have been Jesus Christ, opened his brown paper satchel and we all queued up to make our purchases. These were Charles Atlas sized ounces—six fingers deep, and sticky with resin. At only ten bucks per sandwich baggie, this was the best small-time score I'd ever stumbled upon. Alas, I had only twenty dollars in my bell-bottoms.

The night continued on in this vein until about 3 A.M. Just a bunch of post-Kent State latter-day hippie pretenders taking it light. There was no violence, and the sickness never came. This was the early '70s. I was young.

I was home safe in bed by 3:30.

Later that weekend, since I had the extra 'lid' (which was what an ounce of marijuana was called—no idea why), I thought I'd get a little extravagant. Come Sunday night, with my mom off to her waitressing job at Hof's Hut or Denny's or wherever the hell she was working, I tossed that ounce of pot into a mixing bowl with a box of instant brownie mix, and... *Voila!* I baked 'em, put 'em in the fridge to solid up overnight, then ate the whole pan the next morning in my car on the way to work.

Any experienced pothead will tell you that eating shit is quite a bit different from smoking it. For one thing, there's a delayed reaction before it hits you. Has to work its way through your digestive system. And it sort of creeps up on you at first. You ask yourself, "Wow, is it coming on now?" a few times before you're sure. Or maybe that's because you ALSO smoked a doobie or three because you got impatient waiting for the buzz, and now you're having a hard time distinguishing between the two highs. For some reason, I'm having a little difficulty remembering.

But when those perverted pastries hit you full force, there's no questioning it. Especially when you've got a tum-tum full of relatively chronic cannabis playing sticks on your synapses. I remember the inside of the factory suddenly turning sidewise, which might not have been so bad but for the fact that my knees had surreptitiously made their way round to the backs of my legs. And of course, the cacophony of geometrically shaped pterodactyls shrieking Egyptian at me from my vision's periphery didn't help.

Not to worry. You see, there's a default position that any experienced day-tripper lapses into when the going gets psychotomimetic; it's sort of a stoner's Prime Directive. The word is: MAINTAIN! It's not that difficult. First of all, never call attention to the fact that you're not actually walking, but hovering several inches above the floor...which is writhing with snakes. And when the shop foreman waves his shillelagh at you in a threatening manner, you simply remind yourself that leprechauns went extinct during the last ice age, and there's no gold to be had. Proceed in this manner, smile and nod, nod and smile, and try to spend as much of the day as you can hiding in the bathroom, or out behind the dumpster.

Most important, remember that you're at work, and that you probably can't hide all day. The next best thing is to busy yourself in some far corner with something completely inane. Charade goes a long way when your immediate supervisor is only making four bucks an hour. I remember at some point during the day spending 45 minutes taping down a single corner of tar paper to the floor. Used a whole roll of masking tape and took pride in a job well done.

So I made it through the day, managed to drive my little red '65 Bug with the bad brakes home without mishap, went to bed early... and was still stoned the next morning.

Unfortunately, the residual high wore off rather quickly, leaving me with the usual afterburn. Cotton-brain. I sort of heavy-shoe'd my way through my morning's work, but by midday I felt almost sentient again. Lunchtime came and went. Probably a pastrami sandwich from the Roach Coach. Then it was off to clean up the accumulated fiberglass and asbestos dust coating the factory floor with a nice, cancer-inducing shade of off-white.

Actually, this was my favorite chore. We had this industrial vacuum cleaner, built along the lines of a self-propelled lawnmower. The job was very much like mowing an extremely large but very smooth lawn, in fact. Back and forth, from one end of the factory to the other, I guided my little hovercraft, sucking up the settled detritus of the ever-disgorging chopper guns. All around me, millions of miniscule fiber particles still suspended in the air twinkled in the light of the overhead neons like carcinogenic snowflakes drifting gently in the white noise of my machine's unmuffled two-stroke engine. All the while Emerson Lake and Palmer's cover version of Mussorgsky's "Pictures at an Exhibition" spun on the turntable of my soul.

> *Lead me from tortured dreams,*
> *childhood themes of nights alone;*
> *Wipe away endless years,*
> *childhood tears as dry as stone.*

From seeds of confusion,
illusion's dark blossoms have grown.
Even now in furrows of sorrow
the dance still is sung.

My life's course is guided,
decided by limits drawn
on charts of my past days
and pathways since I was born.

At some point, everything around me faded into a kind of white obscurity. Or perhaps the world was simply absorbed into the rhythm of my walking, my breathing, my being. I'm just not sure.

I carry the dust of a journey
that cannot be shaken away.
It lives deep within me,
for I breathe it every day.

You and I are yesterday's answers;
The earth of the past came to flesh;
Eroded by Time's rivers
to the shapes we now possess.

Come share of my breath and my substance,
and mingle our stream and our times.
In bright, infinite moments,
Our reasons are lost in our rhymes.

I seemed to lose track of everything; yet, somehow, I managed to keep pushing my contraption along, sucking up the fiberglass dust that wasn't making it into my lungs. I felt everything slowing down. Significance and insignificance became one marvelous, ineffable, all-encompassing structure, or maybe just substance. A space opened up above me, and in that space, a single star; and somehow I *knew* that star contained all the past, present and future rolled into one. And I also knew that star was *me*. I knew this with strange certainty. And I knew that I had somehow seen, or felt, or *grokked* God. I was only nineteen.

> There's no end to my life,
> no beginning to my death.
> Death is life!!

I fell to the floor.

I HAD A HARD TIME falling asleep last evening. Nothing particularly urgent pressing on my mind. Just a little bout of insomnia, like I suppose most of us have from time to time. The house was empty and still. The trees outside my window were softly illuminated by moonlight, and even the bees who've recently constructed a hive in the backyard fence seemed bedded down for the night. Then it came—the siren revving up in the distance. Ambulance? Fire truck? The cops? I'm afraid I never did learn to tell the difference, if there even is a difference. I just know it rarely means good news.

When I was twelve and living in Orange County, I was awakened in the middle of the night by a siren. I got out of bed and went to my second story bedroom window. Across the street, in the empty dirt lot where they'd eventually build yet another strip mall, a guy in a golf cart was speeding crazily around in circles, a flashing yellow light on top still plainly visible through the kicked-up dust. I immediately thought to myself, "Oh my God! Robert Kennedy's been assassinated!" Then I went back to bed. That was the early morning hours of June 6, 1968.

Downstairs, Little Voice started howling as the mystery emergency vehicle got closer. They went on in unison like that for a while, as most of the other dogs in the town house complex joined in. Then the noise subsided, and soon it was quiet again. I got to thinking, wondering who'd had the heart attack, or been shot, or lay crushed and broken under the wheels of a jackknifed eighteen wheeler. My older daughter was somewhere in West Hollywood, celebrating Halloween. I wondered how much she'd been drinking. Who she'd be with. If she'd be driving home at three in the morning. And I thought about all the sirens everywhere, speeding to this and that disaster, racing through the darkness under pale moonlight, and of the victims, and the ones they'd leave behind, also victims, and of the dogs, and of the howling. All that howling echoing through the night. I leaned over in my bed, closed the window, and shut my eyes.

It's a wonder the moon never turns its face.

FORTUNATELY, NOBODY WAS paying attention.

Getting back on my feet was only a matter of five or ten seconds; getting back in the game took a few minutes longer. I looked around. Everything seemed the same. Nothing glowed as if illuminated by an internal fire. There were none of the surreal sights and sounds typically associated with my hallucinogenic sojourns. But I was experiencing an overwhelming clarity about...*something*. And that's when I realized that whatever it was that I had experienced was quickly fading away.

Desperately, I tried regaining the high ground by reconstructing the *happening* in my memory, but it was like trying to sink a hook into cotton candy. I'd always been a left-brained sort of guy, but whatever this thing was, it resisted linear conceptualization. There was just nothing to grab hold of. In the end, I had to let it go, and content myself with the afterglow. I was still highly energized. And then...a gift! A shard of retention nested in an axiom:

There is No Time.

Yes! It was so utterly, inexpressibly, inchoately obvious! I went home that afternoon on fire, yelling at my mother, my brothers, and whoever else on the block would listen. "There is no time! Don't you see? There's nothing to worry about! THERE IS NO TIME!" Of course, I had absolutely no idea what this meant, nor do I know now. It was perhaps a decade later that I happened to rediscover the expression in Franlin Merrill Wolfe's little known journal of spiritual transformation, *The Philosophy of Consciousness Without an Object* (or, maybe it was in the companion volume, *Pathways Through to Space*—I can't recall), and later still in some Buddhistic writings describing some aspects of Nirvana. But the actual experience behind these words is forever lost to me, I'm afraid. Not that it matters much anymore. I've moved on.

Speaking of which.

His name was Dieter Linck. Dieter was the resident Jesus freak, though not the pushy sort who's always in your face. He spent his breaks alone, up in the open attic above the offices, eating his lunch and reading his little pocket Bible.

Dieter was a Vietnam vet and an ex-stoner. When Dieter was stoned, he sometimes did things that others might find impulsive. Like having sex with a 13-year-old girl. Or like the time when he was stationed in 'Nam and frying on a high dose of windowpane, when he became convinced he was dead. Consequently believing he was immune from any earthly legal repercussions, he decided to have a little fun with his base commander, spinning a tale about secret agents employed by the Mafia infiltrating the base, spiking the vending machine rations with various poisons and hallucinatory drugs. The C.O. was not amused. Still, Dieter managed to complete his tour of duty, eventually returning stateside with an honorable discharge and no marketable skills.

Did I say Dieter was an *ex*-stoner? Well, he was clean for the most part, though he backslid now and again. It was during one of those backsliding episodes that he tried to unplug one of the chopper guns without turning the machine off, with his safety glasses propped neatly but ineffectually atop his 23-year-old head. He got the job done, alright. Unfortunately, he also got a blast of resin catalyst straight into his left eye. I've seen cans full of fiberglass resin spontaneously burst into flame from having a few ounces too much catalyst mixed in. Dieter's eyeball melted like a plastic army man held over the stove. Fortunately, somebody managed to stop the chemical reaction before the stuff ate up the rest of his face and brain.

I heard this story a year or so after the fact. By the time I met him, Dieter was saving up for a glass eye to fill his empty socket. He'd decided against a lawsuit (wasn't the Christian thing to do), so the company got off scot-free. He told me it was God's way of teaching him a lesson, and that there was a reason for everything. I nodded and went on with my work.

But after my *experience*, I thought if anyone could appreciate what had happened to me, it might be Dieter. After all, it was sort of about God (or so I believed at the time). During the lunch break, I climbed the rickety stairs to Dieter's ersatz crow's nest overlooking the factory floor, and laid it all out for him. He listened quietly to my story, nodding and smiling at all the appropriate places. When I finished, he looked at me with that remaining eye, and said something like, "You've received a precious gift, Jim. God has revealed a great truth to you, for He is indeed timeless, and eternal. God has plans for you, my friend."

Then Dieter opened up. He told me stories about his former decadence and his acceptance of Jesus Christ as his Lord and Savior. Triumphs and failures in his walk with God. Miracles he had witnessed. And so on. All the usual born-again rigmarole; but it was new to me. When he described some of the supernatural stuff that had happened to him, I was blown away. If I'd been older and perhaps a bit wiser, I might have recognized his stories for what they really were (or, at least, for what they seem to be according to the way I interpret such things these days). So many of the stories people tell are confounded by misinterpretation, are layered with hyperbole, superstition and wishful thinking. And the bullshit that comes naturally to us finds purchase in the fertile soil of religion. But I was young. I was inexperienced in the ways of the larger world, and I had no reason to doubt Dieter's tales. Everything he said, I took to be the absolute, literal truth. I lapped it up like nectar. And I found myself interpreting my own seemingly transcendental encounter with the unknown in terms of the God of Abraham, and of His Son and Savior of the World, Jesus Christ.

The kicker came a few weeks later. My boss, the owner of the company, had only recently relocated the plant to Westminster from another building in Costa Mesa, which had been sitting idle for several months. But now the former landlord had lined up some new tenants and there was pressure to get the place completely vacated and cleaned up. Naturally, that job fell on my shoulders. So for a week, I drove out there in the mornings and spent eight hours a day scraping built-up fiberglass residue off the floor with a ten-foot iron bar flattened at one end.

By this time I had come to see virtually everything through the lens of religion. Commonplace routines and minutia seemed to reveal the hand of God—of *my* God, the Christian God. I was drunk with belief. I often imagined that angels, those unseen emissaries of the divine, were all about me—guiding my steps, whilst simultaneously thwarting the attempts of their fallen brethren, likewise invisible, to undermine my burgeoning convictions. Once, after feeding my entire thermos of Spaghetti-O's to a stray dog who'd wandered onto the lot, I became convinced that God had been testing my charity. Judging that I'd passed with flying colors, I gave myself a nice pat on the back, then treated myself to a steak sandwich at the cafe down the street.

It was during my last day at the old factory that the final piece fell into place. I was removing the last big pile of debris into the dumpster outside, when I came across a handmade sign, written in bold felt pen on a large square of cardboard. It said:

> Come now, and let us reason together, saith the LORD: though your sins be as scarlet, they shall be as white as snow; though they be red like crimson, they shall be as wool.
>
> —Isaiah 1:18

I recognized this as likely a piece of Christian propaganda left behind by Dieter. I'd found similar scraps around during my rummaging, though I didn't recognize this particular verse. I'd just recently procured a 'Good News' version of the New Testament, and as far as I knew, the book of Isaiah was not contained therein. Nor was I aware that these fictitious words placed in the mouth of a legendary prophet were, in fact, originally intended for ancient Israelite ears, and were only centuries later hijacked by Christian redactors and turned against the 'people of Moses'—Moses himself being a mythic precursor of Jesus.

All I knew was that God was calling me to Him, and to His Son who had suffered and died on the cross for my sake, and that sending messages through cryptic, easily misinterpreted Bible passages was the way the Creator of the Universe had chosen, in His wisdom, to communicate His intentions to mankind. I also knew that, if I failed to heed His call, when I died, my soul would be cast into a place of eternal pain and torment, forever and ever, amen. I went home that night, got into bed, and prayed for God to forgive my sins through the sacrifice of His Son, Jesus Christ our Lord, and to fill me with His Holy Spirit, that being the third aspect of the Holy Trinity. And He did. Or at least that's the way I saw it at the time.

Nowadays, I see things a bit differently. I don't believe in God. I don't believe in a divine plan, or in a grand cosmic order, or in the concept of 'intrinsic meaning.' I don't believe that life is what you make of it, or that love conquers all. In fact, if I were to encapsulate my feelings about life in one sentence, it would go something like this: 'Life is something that should never have been.'

I wish I were never born. I wish my children had never been born. I wish the sun would explode and crisp us all as we sleep, leaving the Earth a charred, barren, lifeless ball of nothing.

Then, at last, I could rest.

To an Aborted Fetus

Well, I can't say you really missed all that much,
and you were spared an ungodly amount of grief.
All in all, I'd have to say you came out on top—
at least, that is my belief.

And if, perchance, you survived your mortal state,
and are sitting on a cloud in heaven, sipping on something cold, with ice,
then thank your mother that you missed your turn at this dreadful waystation—
'cause they say it's a real bitch, having to be born twice.

The pleasure in this world, it has been said, outweighs the pain; or, at any rate, there is an even balance between the two. If the reader wishes to see shortly whether this statement is true, let him compare the respective feelings of two animals, one of which is engaged in eating the other. The best consolation in misfortune or affliction of any kind will be the thought of other people who are in a still worse plight than yourself; and this is a form of consolation open to every one. But what an awful fate this means for mankind as a whole!

We are like lambs in a field, disporting themselves under the eye of the butcher, who chooses out first one and then another for his prey. So it is that in our good days we are all unconscious of the evil Fate may have presently in store for us—sickness, poverty, mutilation, loss of sight or reason. No little part of the torment of existence lies in this, that Time is continually pressing upon us, never letting us take breath, but always coming after us, like a taskmaster with a whip...

—Arthur Schopenhauer

It's Christmas evening. My mood tends to mirror the drop in the sun's azimuth this time of year. And though it doesn't rise again three days after the solstice in quite the dramatic fashion that's reflected in the Christian resurrection narrative/solar mythology, I'm still glad as hell that the holidays are almost over.

Tomorrow is my younger daughter's 18th birthday. I'll rush home after work to prepare the requested feast of shrimp cocktails, shrimp and cream cheese spread, shrimp linguine, and three kinds of fried shrimp. We'll probably stuff ourselves sick, then cap the evening off with some *Mystery Science Theater 3000*. Then it's back to business, with the slight interruption of the New Year's holiday, which I all but ignore. I suppose I'll make and break a few resolutions, just like everybody else.

Sometimes people ask me, "When did you lose faith in life?" I tell them you can't lose what you never had. Maybe I'm being glib. Or maybe, in plummeting through threshold after threshold of disillusionment, I came to see in a cognizant way what I'd felt all along.

Childhood sucks. Oh, you can cherry-pick your memories and build a fairy castle in Reminiscence Heaven out of the pits if you want to. But I still say you're full of shit if you insist on describing yourself as having been 'a happy child' (rare exceptions notwithstanding, and O how I resent you!). The school playground is a Darwinian trial. Each day brings a new gauntlet to be run, fraught with obstacles, vague and ever-shifting alliances, and very real physical dangers. You dodge budding psychopaths and struggle to secure a safe little niche in the pecking order. I remember once a kid sat on my head out by the tetherball court, and I bit his penis. I was never sure if that singular performance moved me up or down in rank, though I laughed my ass off when they hauled me to the office and I saw the nurse examining him.

And you get knowledge crammed down your throat. At first, it's the three 'R's, those most valuable of basic, practical skills, which about 20% of American teenagers somehow fail to attain after 12 years of schooling. Somewhere along the way, other subjects get piled on: social studies, history, geography, foreign and domestic literatures, science, and levels of higher mathematics that become increasingly divorced from any reality almost any kid is ever going to experience. This is the mandated course.

Naturally, school isn't a child's entire life. At some point late in the day, they send you on your way back home, but not before they pack your arms (backpacks, nowadays) full of heavy books and homework assignments. Just their little way of prolonging the agony. And you do it, or you don't. Then you try to grab a little time for yourself before dinner and bedtime, so you can get up and do it all over again the next day, the next month, the next year.

And what's the carrot at the end of this pedagogical stick? Why, you'll graduate! They'll give you a little piece of paper that says 'You've arrived!' Only you haven't actually arrived. Because now, if you really want to be somebody, you've got to go to college, and do it all over again. That way, after four, or six, or eight, or twelve years, you'll graduate AGAIN, and they'll give you ANOTHER piece of paper that says 'Now you've REALLY made it!' And if you're lucky, provided you chose a financially lucrative major instead of something you were actually interested in, you might just earn enough to eventually pay off all those student loans, and then you'll finally be free and clear to...

To *what?* What, precisely, are we being prepared to do? It can't be about personal happiness, since it seems most of us spend half our waking hours—at least!—doing things we'd rather not be doing but for the required income our efforts generate, and the other half recuperating from those labors so we'll be able to rise in the morning and start all over again. On our days off, we sleep in if we're lucky (sleep: the living version of being dead), and then we spend the rest of the day doing the work we didn't have time to do during the week when we were 'at work.'

That's pretty much the whole story for the first 60 or 70 years of life, if we manage to make it that far. After that, it's retirement in bodies worn down to the nubs, a flurry of medical care at the end, and then death. Back to where we started, which was precisely nowhere.

Why?

So that the next generation can come along behind, and do the same thing.

Why?

Because the human race MUST go on!

Why?

Um...God's will?

No.

Uh...circle of life?

Nope.

Fluoride in the water?

That's another subject.

THE HARDEST THING about putting down a family pet is telling the kids about it. It's doubly hard when your atheism doesn't allow for a Doggy Heaven. When I informed my daughter that I'd soon be having our 14-year-old Lhasa Apso, Barney, put to sleep, she looked me straight in the eye, and said, "But, if that's all life comes down to, then it's all just stupid. What's the point?"

What do you suppose I said to her?

I SPENT MOST of my twenties in a religious cult.

My mom was dating this guy named Leo, some dude she met in a dance club in Buena Park (he's dead now; clubbed over the head with a lead pipe, repeatedly, in his own house by some punk he'd pissed off for god knows what reason). Anyhow, she was hard up for money, trying to keep a roof over herself and her five sons after her divorce. Leo knew some hippie named Rich, and Rich needed a place to stay. Within the week, he was moved into what had formerly been my father's den, right next to my bedroom. This arrangement turned out to be convenient for all of us. Mom received some rent money to help with the monthly bills. Rich got a place to live. And as for me? Well, I got a next door neighbor who scored me the purest, mind meltingest lysergic acid diethylamide in Orange County.

Fortunately, Rich was a heavy-duty acidhead as well, and was usually more interested in securing a copilot than a customer. His penchant for serial tripping made me look like a piker. I remember him dosing on a dozen hits of windowpane to my one, yet I was the guy who had to ride shotgun. Still, the excesses took their toll. Rich was fucked up. A burnout. One time when he was driving we picked up a hitchhiker, got on the freeway, then Rich casually removed the steering wheel—which happened to be unbolted from the tree at the time—handed it to the guy in the backseat, and asked him to go ahead and drive.

But he gave me free dope, and I liked him.

After my religious conversion, I taped up my remaining dope and paraphernalia in a Swisher Sweets cigar box, tossed it all in the trash, and said goodbye to the evils of drug induced euphoria. Jesus was to be my only high from then on. At least for the next eight years or so. When I clued Rich into my new lifestyle and allegiances, he took to it with good grace, unlike some of my other acquaintances. Not really that surprising, since his mother was a fundamentalist Christian.

It wasn't long before I was attending regular services on Sundays and Wednesday nights with Rich's mom at Melodyland in Anaheim, a non-denominational church across the street from Disneyland. Agatha was cool in a ditzy, emotionally overcharged sort of way. She was of the 'charismatic' stripe of fundamentalist Christianity; lots of singing, crying, praying out loud or in tongues. Since I didn't have any experience in the ways of the spirit, I took all this rigmarole as part of God's mysterious ways. And I took Agatha's misinformed exegeses, as well as her revelatory utterances whilst in the throes of prophetic ecstasy, as gospel. This was all new territory to me. When in Rome, y'know?

Things went along like this for six months or so. Everything in my life was very God-focused. Due to my naive but effective evangelical fervor, I even managed to recruit a few friends along the way. Rich was one of them.

We used to gather after services in a coffeshop nearby. Some nights, nine or ten of us sat around a table, holding hands, saying grace aloud with utter conviction. Seems quite pharisaical in retrospect, and I'm sure the waitresses thought we were nuts. Like other adherents to the charismatic/Pentecostal brand, we were really into the end-times stuff as supposedly outlined in the Book of John's Revelation as interpreted by Hal Lindsay and company. (Did I mention we were idiots?) We were constantly on the lookout for signs from God, both of the apocalyptic kind, as well as those concerning our personal 'walks' with Him. Our conversations were peppered with watchwords and buzz phrases. We spoke of 'God's will,' and 'when Jesus comes' to take us away in 'The Rapture.'

Needless to say, such a confluence of portentous energies carries its own backlash. Because here's the truth of the matter, folks. There IS NO GOD! Jehovah is just another middle eastern thunder deity, Jesus is the umpteenth incarnation of an agriculture mythologist's wet dream (Jesus is coming!), and the Holy Spirit is just…well, he's just *nothing*. He got tacked on as an afterthought at this or that holy council of Rome once upon a time, probably because people like the number three for some reason. That's also the story of pretty much every other religion that's ever existed. Just change the names, and play the game, amen. I think most of us in this so-called post-Enlightenment age know this deep down. But there's always this internal conflict going on between what common sense tells us, and what the society around us tells us is so, including all the crap that's drilled into us as kids.

The results of this interior dissonance are two. Doubt and fear. You try to squelch it, maybe drown it out with prayer or self-flagellation, but the whispers invariably demand attention.

"What if there is no God?"

"What if I've chosen the wrong God?"

"What if I'm on the wrong path, going against His will?"

"What if I'm not trying hard enough?"

And you're told that's the Devil talking to you, which actually means you're on the right path since Satan's going to all this bother in the first place. And sometimes you're assuaged by that facile explanation, except that voice sounds an awful lot like your own. Should old Beelzebub really sound that much like you? And if so, how can you separate your thoughts from his, or from God's, for that matter? And over all this confusion hangs the threat of eternal damnation if you should discover your mistake too late. Believe me or don't, but this is the boiling madness that foments a lot of the fire-and-brimstone zeal you see in those preachers on TV.

So one evening during a break in my Thursday night Bible class, I stepped outside to get some air. The doubts had been battering against my faith pretty heavily the last few weeks. I felt my resolve crumbling out from beneath me, and I desperately needed some answers—or at least some suave apologetic salving. Across the street in the Grand Hotel's glass elevator, I could see a couple of guys faking a mugging; some puerile theater for those few of us in the street who might happen to be looking their way. But I also saw it as a metaphor for the struggle going on in my own head. Maybe even a tussle between the Powers of Light and Darkness for my very soul.

It was just about this time that a dwarfish, misshapen fiend with a maggot-infested red beard and a speech impediment came skulking around the corner. I should have known better, but I let him engage me in conversation. Beguiling me in the ancient tongue of his demon clan, he soon won me over with his lies disguised as wisdom. A few weeks later, I left my family, friends and most of what few possessions I owned, and hit the road with him and his devilish brood, one of whom I later married, and bore children with.

Well, actually...

His name was Andy, and he was an itinerant preacher traveling around the country for Jesus in his '68 Dodge pickup. Accompanying him were his family, and the young woman who was to become my future wife. Theirs was a special mission, a 'last days' push by God Himself to get His Church in final order, and ready for the Apocalypse that was right around the corner. Andy fancied himself an apostle, a preacher's preacher, if you will. Like most cult leaders, his line to God was just a little bit clearer than the rest. He was God's wingman, and by extension, anyone else who was part of his little tribe became part of Heaven's inner circle, privy to all the really important stuff.

Now, think back to my apprehensive mindset at the time, and try to imagine the surge of relief and hope that I, James Crawford, experienced. I had been chosen by the Creator of the universe to be part of His special, elite force. I was one of the chosen. The elect. It was as if I were St. Matthew of ancient Israel being called by Jesus Himself to follow, and ultimately to lead. How could I have refused?

So, sometime in March of 1976, I packed my little green suitcase into the old blue Dodge, said goodbye to my mom and four little brothers, and drove east, straight into the rising nightfall of my destiny.

And then what happened?

The usual, I suppose. There was brainwashing. There were bizarre rituals. There was emotional and physical abuse, and all the craziness the word 'cult' is meant to imply. I spent nearly eight years—most of my twenties, for chrissake—believing in and propagating an ancient myth better left to the trash heap of gods who have outlived their usefulness, all the while, kowtowing to a cruel, ignorant hick straight out of Tobacco Road. A man who was barely literate, but who knew enough godspeak to keep us all on leashes woven of naïveté and craven fear. I will forever be ashamed of those days—for my participation, for my cowardice, and for the utter waste of my time.

Yet there was a silver lining. I'll get to it.

Thᴇʏ sᴀʏ ᴡᴇ ʟɪᴇ an average of three times for every ten minutes of conversation. I'm not sure where they got those numbers. They're probably making them up. I've met enough pathological liars to suspect the spectrum is flanged, at least, at one end.

Nevertheless, it would seem that the human propensity for telling lies—be they of the little white, hyperbolic, or bald-faced variety—is one of the more distinguishing characteristics of the species. Or is it? Most behavioral scientists nowadays would acknowledge that our prevarication tendencies have a broad and deep evolutionary heritage. There seem to be countless examples in the natural world of species that use camouflage and mimicry to achieve Darwinian ends. Deception has its advantages.

And when you consider the exponentially more complex world of the abstract human mindscape nested inside the almost infinitely entangled matrix of communal interactions that make up a culture, one can see how deceptive strategies could go apeshit. Ever been to the Vatican?

Perhaps our tendency toward deception evolved in service to the demands of an earlier time, when self-preservation was paramount, almost to the exclusion of any other considerations. Whatever its natural history, it is curious that lying remains a source of lingering tension and unease, a trait at odds with our rational nature. Ostensibly eschewed while privately practiced, lying is thus seldom accorded the status of virtue. But does even a collective nod toward principled truth-telling tell us something about the course we're on? Something positive?

I believe it does.

Earlier I talked about empathy, that cultivated assemblage of human sensibilities which allows us to extend our sense of self, and thus our concerns, outward to include other lives. The degree to which we're able to do this separates us from other life forms, though I don't doubt that some correlative attributes extend further down the evolutionary chain in some fashion, albeit to a lesser extent. But empathy, or vicarious emotion, is just half of the story. The other half is our ability to reason. It is the quality of human reasoning, with all that term infers and implies—analytical thinking, logical processing, deduction, induction, abduction and so on—which has made us the dominant species on this planet. And for all we know, in the whole universe.

Reason has served us well. Mostly because it helps us get at the truth of things, which can be a great advantage in a reality where mistakes can exact great costs. But who says we always want to know the truth? In real life, fiction is often more convenient, more comfortable, and frankly, more marketable. So lying, too, has served us—efficiently, if not well. The human propensity to deceive has been refined and cultivated and internalized precisely because it's such a damned useful trait. Though moral idealists would be loath to admit it, lying is probably a predominant factor in the continuing survival of the human species. But that's the problem. Lying, especially the self-deceptive kind that gets fed back into the cultural machinery in ten thousand ways, is serving a survival instinct that butts straight up against what our reason-informed empathy (or is it the other way around?) is telling us. Namely, that life is ultimately malevolent, and should not go on.

I know that last statement is a lot to swallow. But it is my strongly held opinion that most folks believe there's something profoundly wrong with life. This sense of wrongness emerges not only from our personal experience of pain, loss, and futility, but also from the dim knowledge of the accumulated sufferings of the world; from the onus of awareness burning at the core of our empathic selves.

This awareness puts us on edge. So we develop coping strategies. Biases. We focus, desperately, on the positive. We seek solace in lies, such as those embodied in religion and other imaginary side streets that we can duck into when ugly truths come to block our rose-tinted view.

Yet a grim truth haunts us at all turns. It is reflected in the tale of Noah's flood and the coming of the New Jerusalem. It is resonant in the Buddha's basic maxim that all life is suffering, the knowledge of which is to be overcome through detachment, or in the blackened glass of the addict's crack pipe, or simply in the nine-to-fiver's 72-inch plasma television screen.

The key word is *escape*. Get me OUT of this fucking place!

Back to the cult.

About a month after the 'family' was officially disbanded—though some of us still lived together—another member and I decided to go fishing. We drove north for a bit to a little stretch of the Rogue River where we'd had some luck before. Donning our chest-waders, we shuffled out over the algae-slickened bedrock with fly rods in hand, and spent a pleasant couple of hours beneath Oregon's summer sky amidst the midges, and the rainbow trout. I might have even caught one.

Mark and I were still Christians at this time. However, the disbandment of the cult seemed to have loosened us in some way. The changes we were experiencing went unspoken for the most part, as we had been conditioned to keep doubts and controversial viewpoints to ourselves. That's what religious dogma is all about. Don't question. Just accept. And so we had accepted, for almost eight years. But with the ousting of the slave master, all us vassals began feeling just the slightest bit cocky. Each of us, in his own way, had begun entertaining serious questions. Our minds were churning with alternative visions of what life was about, and of possibilities seditious and delicious.

But old habits born of swift and cruel retribution are hard to break.

On the way home in the car, the conversation circled the subject that was on both our minds, but neither of us could quite summon up the courage to come in for a landing. That is, until one of us said something like, "What if the Bible really isn't the Word of God? In fact, what if God was just made up by these guys who wrote the books in the first place?"

I think it was me who asked the question. I remember Mark's jaw dropping slightly. He stared quietly at me for several seconds.

In retrospect, the picture of a couple of grown men having this conversation seems on the far side of ludicrous; but there we were, and there it is. We both realized, I think, how we had been hoodwinked. There was no God. Jesus was not Lord. Nor had he died for our sins. Nor was the Holy Spirit watching us, or reading our thoughts or judging us. Nor did Satan whisper dark heresies to tempt us from the fold. We were alone.

Both of us started to cry. And then to laugh. And then to cry again. Two grown men.

And there's the silver lining. The day I rejected God was the day I was truly born again. It was also the day when I began to question everything, including the presuppositional illusions and delusions that help us get through the day, without ever asking why the fuck we're doing it in the first place.

Why do we continue to create life when all life is condemned to suffering and death? That's the question that would, in time, rear up from the abyss. Once I hooked it, I couldn't let it go. I've since had time to consider the reasons, one by one. And I have concluded that the reasons are bad. That they fail to provide sufficient justification for otherwise good people to do a bad thing.

No one should ever have children.

Alas, none of us are purely rational animals, and the most reasonable among us still do stupid things from time to time. For instance, I had children. Understanding they would suffer. Realizing the chance that they might suffer horribly. Knowing they would die. Why did I do it? For the same bad faith reasons any otherwise intelligent and caring people do it.

I try not to be too hard on myself. Like everyone else, I was programmed in countless ways to fulfill the Prime Directive of human existence—'Be ye fruitful, and multiply!' It's tough to lean into that particular wind, especially when the masses keep blowing it your way. But if we care, and if we care enough to think the issue all the way through to the implacable black heart of the matter, then I believe reason can prevail.

I said earlier that hope is my enemy. I stand by that statement, but I suppose I'm holding a little to the side here. Call it hair of the dog.

I'VE HAD SOME WEIRD health problems in my life. My stomach goes south on me every year or so, generally for an average of five days, during which time I suffer excruciating pain, to the point where I'm literally sobbing. Scares the hell out of my kids. It put me in the hospital once for six weeks. I had two surgeries, though they never did solve the problem. In fact, most of my doctors thought I was going to die. My older daughter was only two months old at the time. I don't know what she thought.

When I was 40, I had a sudden case of vertigo while I was out in the garage building Christmas presents for the girls. It got worse and worse over an hour or so until I wound up in the emergency room of the county hospital in Riverside. Some might remember that as the place where, once in the early '90s, some 'mysterious fumes' wafted out of a cancer patient's body cavity, causing several nurses to collapse. All around the world, doctors speculated about what had happened. Some blamed mass hysteria. I don't think the issue was ever settled to anybody's satisfaction. Shortly thereafter a nutcase crept over to an old man in the next bed and bit his penis clean off. Then he hanged himself. Eventually they moved County out to a new building in Moreno Valley and tore the old place down. I think I have a brick from the demolition in my closet somewhere. Souvenir.

After waiting a couple of hours for a doctor, and seeing none on the horizon, I shrugged my shoulders and went back home.

I figured I'd probably die in bed that night. I didn't, though I experienced continuing sporadic dizziness, as well as weird muscle spasms and fatigue for the next couple of months. These 'symptoms' occasionally resurfaced to a lesser extent for many years. I learned to work around it, which is pretty fucking impressive considering I was a construction painter, often working on tall ladders and hi-rise scaffolds dangling a couple hundred feet above the ground. You do what you have to.

About five years ago, I discovered quite by accident that my blood pressure was 260/138. All the time. I was told this was not good, but since I had no money and no medical insurance, I let it go. The matter came up later when I couldn't pass the medical requirements for a construction job I was applying for. I stayed on as a temp and tried to get the pressure managed through diet and exercise, but it didn't budge. Finally I tried meds. They worked, but not well enough, and they were costing me three hundred bucks a month, so I gave them up pretty quickly. My truck eventually crapped out on me, so I couldn't get back out to that job anyway. So much the better. I was on an assembly line manufacturing mobile homes, and I'd gotten tired of having roofers drop tools on my head, and of getting shot in the back with nail guns. I'm particular that way.

After that, I got a job close to home as a cook at the fast-food restaurant where my daughter worked (thank god, she's moved on to better things). I kept exercising, riding my bike, trying to eat reasonably healthy, and I eventually forgot all about the blood pressure. Then, about a year and a half ago, I started experiencing fatigue, as well as some pain in my upper back. I thought I might just be catching something, and pushed my way through it. But then it got to the point where I couldn't walk fifty feet in a straight line without feeling like I was going to collapse. I drove myself to County General (the new one), and they checked me in. They never did seem very clear on precisely what had happened, but eventually chalked it all up to an 'episode' related to my blood pressure. They wrote me a bunch of prescriptions, helped me get on the state's medically indigent program, and wrote off my bills as a loss. I kept on the meds, and slowly I got better. I did have one relapse that sent me back to the hospital for a few days. But again I recovered. Since then I've had no further problems. Nothing serious, anyway. Life goes on.

My first child was born in the summer of 1987; a daughter. Hers was a natural birth, on time with no complications (her mother might differ on that). I assisted with that birth, to the extent that subdued, panicky reassurances offered through clenched teeth may be counted as assistance. And when I saw the top of that wet, matted head emerge from the birth canal, no one on earth could have convinced me that I wasn't witnessing a genuine miracle. It was the first time, and perhaps the last, that I ever cried tears of pure, unadulterated joy.

My second child, also a daughter, was born in the winter of 1990. My wife announced the conception to me with a big smile, and a card inscribed by proxy, which read something like, "Hello, Daddy. I'll be here in December...I love you." My response was lackluster. My wife's reaction would best be described as incomprehension tinged with sadness, and once again I wept—this time, in private. For her. For us.

I felt like a criminal.

It was a visceral response, of course. I managed to affect the old game face in fairly short order, though I don't think I ever apologized. Straightforward dissembling was mostly beyond me by then. But I managed to skirt conversation reflecting the ever-widening hole I felt growing at my center, as I did my best to play the role of the supportive husband and father. It wasn't too hard. After all, insufficient hopefulness in the face of irremediable knowledge is the backbone of the universal human experience, is it not? Dread is just another emotion; it passes like all emotions pass. Like the chill you get sometimes when a cloud passes overhead. You get distracted for a moment, but then the sun comes out again, and you go on about your business under a mostly blue sky. It only gets complicated when you begin to suspect that blue skies are the real distraction.

Our second experience with childbirth didn't come off nearly as hitchless as the first. To begin with, the baby was two weeks late. Ultimately, the doctor deemed it necessary to induce childbirth. I sat bedside and observed as he manually broke my wife's water, the released amniotic fluid immediately soaking the hospital bedsheets. After that, it was simply a waiting game. The doctor assured us that it wouldn't be more than a few hours. In fact, he convinced us to change the middle name from Nicole to Noel, it being late morning on Christmas Day. Seemed like a pretty cool idea at the time.

But the waiting stretched on, continuing into the afternoon. I kept darting out to the parking lot to smoke, at one point wandering over to the 7-Eleven across the street for a magazine. (This was the same 7-Eleven where years earlier a friend of mine from high school had been shot dead in the face behind the counter during a holdup. I heard the punks were laughing about it when the cops caught them. You know how those stories go.) I settled on a copy of *Newsweek*. The cover write-up highlighted a newly coined phrase that was then sweeping the country—'Political Correctness.'

When I returned, things were pretty much the same. I settled into my vigil, offering comfort where I could as my wife drifted in and out, whilst reading my magazine and muttering under my breath about the sorry state of free speech.

Sometime during the late afternoon, the monitor attached to the baby's skull inside my wife's womb started beeping, and suddenly the room was packed with nurses. One of them crammed her hand up to her wrist into my wife's vagina, freaking me the fuck out. This was a procedure which was to be repeated several more times into the late evening. Seems the baby's heart kept stopping, and the method by which they got it kick-started again was by massaging her scalp (still beats the hell out of me how that works). Both of us were pretty wiped out by all the drama. I think it was around midnight when the doctor finally gave up on the idea of a natural birth. Neither of us fought him very hard. At this point, we just wanted the ordeal to be over.

So early on the morning of December 26th, our second daughter was delivered by C-section. Everybody breathed a sigh of relief.

After the delivery, they sewed my wife up and doped her into a coma, then they put my newborn daughter into an incubator. (She'd managed to pick up an infection during all the goings on; it would be a week before they finally released her to us.) Since I had no further purpose to serve, the staff finally persuaded me to be on my way. I think it was around 4 AM when I stumbled into my house. I remember half-watching some godawful Dustin Hoffman movie on TV, in between periods of spacing out on the lava lamp my brother got me for Christmas. I must have fallen asleep in my chair at some point, though I'm not really sure when.

Each one of us was harmed by being brought into existence. That harm is not negligible, because the quality of even the best lives is very bad—and considerably worse than most people recognize it to be. Although it is obviously too late to prevent our own existence, it is not too late to prevent the existence of future possible people. Creating new people is thus morally problematic.

—David Benatar

In his book, *Better Never To Have Been: The Harm Of Coming Into Existence*, in the chapter entitled "Why Coming Into Existence Is Always A Harm," South African professor of philosophy David Benatar posits a fundamental asymmetry embedded in the very fabric of living existence, one which he believes exposes a fatal flaw in the common intuition that bringing new life into the world is an ultimately benign or worthwhile endeavor. The first part of the equation goes like this:

1. The presence of pain is bad.
2. The presence of pleasure is good.

Taken together, these two statements represent half of an argument aimed at addressing the largely unexamined notion that life is intrinsically desirable. I say notion, but maybe it would be more accurate to call it a nearly universal presumption. At least, that's the way it seems on the face of things. Certainly antinatalism is one of those taboo subjects, which, like religion, is broached amongst mixed company only with a certain degree of judiciousness. Like wondering aloud about Jesus Christ's masturbatory habits, it won't win you many friends. And in some circles, it might stir up a flurry of ill will.

I found myself in such a position a few years ago at work. Several young, female coworkers were waxing on about their future plans, all of which included the bearing of children. At some point in the conversation I was moved to interject.

"Have any of you ever thought it might not be such a good idea to have kids?"

"What do you mean? Don't you like kids?"

"Well, yeah...most of them, anyway. That's not really the point, though. Take you, Yvonne. You're not married. Your boyfriend just tried to commit suicide. Your daughter is three years old and has already had two surgeries for birth defects, with more to come. You work a minimum wage job. You have no education, no money, no car, and no definite upward prospects in your immediate future. Doesn't at least part of you wish you'd thought twice before you conceived? And don't any of you others think about such things? Not at all?"

Talk about sucking the air out of the room! My points were met with a few resistant *yeah buts*, and as everybody drifted back to their work stations, one girl turned back to me and remarked, somewhat disconsolately, "You know, Jim, I'd always thought you were a nice guy."

Anyway. Where were we? Ah, the first two axioms of professor Benatar's asymmetry. At first glance, nothing seems particularly controversial here. Pain is bad. Pleasure is good. Can anyone reasonably deny these assertions? Or are we getting ahead of ourselves? Certainly there must exist some foundational principle, or set of principles, some presuppositional takeoff point from which such positively stated maxims derive, no? We shall discover such a point in the ethical doctrine of hedonism. Mind you, I'm not referring to some caricature of self-indulgent Bohemianism, but rather to a strict philosophical rendering of the word. My Webster's defines hedonism as

> *The ethical doctrine that pleasure, variously conceived of in terms of happiness of the individual or of society, is the principal good and the proper aim of action.*

Naturally, questions arise concerning scope, nuance and applicability. How happy should we be, and at what sacrifice? Does everyone deserve to be happy? Can true pleasure even be known without its opposite to provide contrast? Is immediate pleasure what's most important, or should we be looking for a more encompassing, long-term sense of well-being? All interesting questions, but not particularly important here. For my purposes, any mix of the above will do. Suffice it to say that the maximization of pleasure IS the defining hedonistic imperative. And though I'd agree that the particular characteristics, breadth, depth, as well as the preferred balance struck between these facets will surely vary from person to person, I think we can paint some broad descriptive strokes that few people would dispute. But before we go there, we probably should address the other side of the existential ledger, since that's the way Professor Benatar set it up.

Let's talk about pain.

Why is pain 'bad'? Certainly, taken on its face this proposition is at least theoretically falsifiable. In fact, I'd go so far as to say that it's blatantly false; that is, within a certain arena of experience. For is not pain a necessity, a biological distress signal honed through billions of years of evolution? Pain is a teacher, instructing us through trial and error that it's NOT OK to thrust our hands into the fire (the classic example), and that it generally works against our better self-interest to swallow sharp, pointy things. This is a rather common riposte I've encountered in discussions about antinatalism, and concerning Mr. Benatar's arguments in particular. But pain justified as an organic pedagogical mechanism fails on a couple of fronts. At least, it does when used as an apologetic outside the strictly utilitarian function.

First consider the fact that, in most cases, pain outlives its functional usefulness. Oh, it's all well and good in teaching me

NOT to touch the hot stove. And even though I'm 53 years old and learned the lesson of hot stove touching long ago, I guess I can still rationalize pain's existence as a negatively reinforcing reminder. Sort of like a piece of thread (or piano wire, as the case may be) tied around the index finger. Yet we are left with the reality that pain often lingers on after its practical value has been tapped. A minor inconvenience when I accidentally blister my pinkie on the 425 degree quesadilla iron at work. Something qualitatively more to the burn victim who has to undergo months of therapeutic skin scrapes.

A second limitation to the pain as stern-but-caring-schoolmaster argument is the undeniable fact that, in the end, pain will NOT pull us out of the fire. All of us will eventually succumb to that which pain is trying to ultimately save us from—namely, irremediable injury, or loss of bodily function unto death. It logically follows that pain, while admittedly serving some contextually useful purposes (while also acknowledging the aforementioned cross-purposes), is, like all utilitarian functions, of only relative and partial value. This truth cuts across the grain of those critics who would imply that pain has *intrinsic value*; a phrase I find utterly meaningless in most if not all cases, but especially as employed to justify pain. Almost none of us really buys this gambit, anyway. Apart from the few who might cultivate it as an experiential exclamation point punctuating certain sadomasochistic preferences, pain is merely a by-product to be alleviated. Let's square up here—we go to great lengths to avoid it; or, once encountered, to get rid of it as quickly as possible. It's even a crime to inflict too much of it, under most circumstances. The presence of pain...is bad.

It might be useful here to distinguish the concept of pain as a functional, reflexive intermediary between the biological mechanism and its environment (or as an alarm system monitoring the inner workings of the mechanism itself) from what might be called *existential* pain, which is to say, *suffering*. The terms are often used synonymously, but I think most of us would acknowledge differences in both resonance and quality. I think it's fair to say that suffering both encompasses the sensations of bodily discomfort brought on by injury, disease, and a host of other functional disorders, while at the same time transcending them by adding a psychological thickness to the issue. This isn't an attempt at some metaphysical duality statement. Being something of a pragmatic naturalist (except on Tuesdays, when I'm a solipsist), I don't have a big problem with identifying the mental realm as an extension of the physical one. Still, we live in a world of impressions based on a probably inescapable paring of the apple—my clever little way of saying that brain states divide the world up to make for easier digesting. Thus we have a 'physical' world as opposed to a 'mental' one, and I don't suffer any grave discomfiture in seeing things that way. Maybe someday my recalcitrant Zen enlightenment will take, and then I'll finally grok the unity of it all. (Actually, I hope that's not the case, and I'll explain why further along.)

For present purposes, I'm just trying to point out what we all know. The fact is that physical pain is actually brain pain, which amounts to psychic pain, which is a lot more than simply physical pain—which, in the end, is just a referent for one aspect of psychological pain, which is suffering. Hard to say with a mouthful of cashews, but the underlying reality is easily recognizable to any half-sentient creature. The many and varied descriptive terms for suffering are familiarly ubiquitous: discomfort, distress, anguish, misery, fear, loathing, longing, hunger, agony, despair, desolation, worry, hatred, depression, grief, sadness, anxiousness—these and a host of others, on top of the more narrowly defined, physically oriented aches, pains and stab wounds one is pressed to avoid. All this, along with all the little imaginable corollaries entailed, informs the phenomenology of the negative human experience that Professor Benatar is alluding to when he posits his first axiom, "The presence of pain is bad."

Moving on to the second axiom: The presence of pleasure is good.

Why is pleasure good? I suppose before we attempt to answer that, we should try to discover what we mean by 'pleasure.' Or is this something too obvious to even go into? Pistachio nut ice cream, a warm summer eve's breeze, puppies and paychecks and blow jobs (oh my!), mud baths, all-night karaoke slams (well, for some), a good read, a good movie, barreling down a hill on your 21-speed, midnight Chinese leftovers, a walk in the park, a night on the beach, a rainy afternoon when all you have to do is lie on the couch and listen to it hit the window, the voice of a friend, the kindness of strangers, the chance to do something selfless with absolutely no skin off your nose, getting a kite so far up there that the string seems suspended by nothing, sinking a hook shot from half court, getting someone to believe an outrageously ridiculous story just for kicks (I was merciless with my kids on this one), good neighbors, good beer, good movies, bad movies that are so bad they somehow become good. All these and much, much more contribute to the personal enjoyment, satisfaction, and a sense of fulfillment that might fall under the umbrella term 'pleasure,' or one of several equivalent terms, however nuanced.

But why is it good? When asking this question, it's tempting to seek out some standard for goodness from the stratosphere, a stamp of approval from on high that might endorse our personal inclinations as lining up with some transcendental template. For some, that means 'God' as well as all the dogma implied in the term. Depending on the creed and its specific doctrines, seeking goodness might, and ofttimes does, cause someone's preferences to deviate sharply from those things he might otherwise find personally pleasurable. This brand of cognitive dissonance can lead down one of two paths. One can either repress certain tendencies under threat of punishment—sort of the Sword of Damocles approach—or one's own emotional nature can become transformed to line up with the new, authoritarian guidelines. On further reflection, I doubt these two approaches are mutually exclusive, and are probably embodied in all of us who aren't archetypal hedonists.

For those less deistically inclined, secular humanists for example, the question isn't about how we're supposed to feel as defined by some cosmic lawgiver (take your pick), but about how we DO feel—or, perhaps more precisely, how we WANT to feel. From this starting point comes the institutionalization of laws and regulations designed to strike a happy medium of personal happiness across the societal playing field... in theory, though we all know how ideals fare in the street of practical application.

Often it happens that human predilections are assumed to be more universal than they actually are. They are granted deontological status akin to holy writ, then force-fed to the refractory holdouts with a paternalism right out of the book of Job. This is the way it will always be, to some extent. Concurrent with our wish to understand the human condition through over-simplification is our tendency to ground human desire and behavior in 'natural rights.' Such 'rights' are often gleaned, reasonably, from empathic awareness of the human condition. Where proponents get off track is when they assume these rights are imbedded in the very fabric of existence, like the laws of gravity or motion. To really get a grip on the fundamental difference between laws and rights, one only has to ask: when was the last time anybody had to enforce gravity? To understand human rights as something above and beyond a status granted by authority—or, conversely, the refusal of authority to interfere in what people want to do—is simply an attempt to elevate authority to the abstract. In a sense, it's the canonization of the human condition. "This is it! This is good! There's nothing more to be said!" It's not so much a reflection of reality, as an attempt to make reality conform to a particular moral structure to settle ontological questions. And, of course, to help grease the skids of administrative tasks.

So when I endorse the assertion that "the presence of pleasure is good," I'm not pleading to some definition of goodness delivered from a mountaintop, nor from some indwelling numen whispering dicta from behind the veils of intuition. Ultimately, what's good is what I like. No more, and no less. Whether the question concerns gods who punish worlds because ancient ancestors ate the wrong fruit, or simply the taste of ice cream, it all comes down to me and my personal preferences.

And when I argue that having children is wrong, I'm not obstinately shouting down Jehovah's 'be fruitful and multiply' moral imperative from the other end of the table. I'm simply making a case extrapolated from my own human sensibilities, believing that others share many of those sensibilities, and that if they follow the course of my arguments they might come to see that promoting child-bearing actually works against their own emotional self interests.

On to the other half of Professor Benatar's proposed asymmetry after these important messages...

Hey, there! Feeling run down? Overworked? Fearful about the future? All those news stories about war, disease, and disaster making you wonder if life is what it's really cracked up to be? Stomach in a knot? Can't sleep? Hitting those prescription meds a little heavy lately? Looking for a way out of that depressive mind-state? Need a dose of hope? Well, have I got the answer for you! HAVE KIDS! A passel of 'em! Hand off that crippling psychological burden of yours to the next generation, so you can tell yourself, "It'll all work out. If not for me, then for them, or for their kids, or..."

And by all means, encourage your children to do the very same thing! Teach them to spread the breeding fever to all their friends! Spin that storyline! Disperse that ennui into a make-believe future where fairies are real, where nobody ever gets sick or dies, and where dreams DO come true!

Eventually.

Now then. Where were we? Oh, yes:

> 3. The absence of pain is good, EVEN if that good is not enjoyed by anyone.

> 4. The absence of pleasure is NOT bad UNLESS there is somebody for whom this absence is a deprivation.

This is the other half of Professor Benatar's asymmetry, where the real weight of his argument rests, and where things get tricky. While it is hardly controversial to state that pain is bad while pleasure is good, our footing is less sure when attributing values usually reserved for existent, sensate beings, e.g., people and other living creatures, to nonexistent, hypothetical beings whose ethical relevance resides *in potentia*. A few objectors have tried to make hay of this, even going so far as to claim that absolutely no moral valuations concerning the unborn—or preexistent—can be justified at all. But is this really a reasonable position to take? Let's do a thought experiment.

Imagine you live in a kingdom ruled by an all-powerful, incredibly sadistic and brutal king. Upon each child's second birthday, he or she is delivered to the royal castle to be thoroughly tortured purely for the entertainment of the king and his entourage. The child is administered to by court physicians throughout these proceedings, so as to keep him/her from actually dying. In this way, the entertainment can be protracted, sometimes for years! No child ever escapes this fate, for the King's spies are EVERYWHERE!

Under such circumstances, is it truly beyond the bounds of rationality to at least consider the future welfare of a child who does not, as yet, exist? During the potential parents' conversations regarding the wisdom of bearing a child under such vile circumstances, surely the natural question to arise might be something along the lines of "My dearest husband, do you really think bringing a child into this world, at this time, would be a GOOD thing to do?" (the 'good' referring to the future state of the not-yet-existent child, of course).

Am I missing something? Where's the philosophical conundrum? Of COURSE *not* being born into such a world is better than *being* born into such a world, by pretty much any ethical mensuration you wish to apply (notwithstanding some overriding religious edicts, perhaps wielded by pronatal absolutists). I use 'ethical' with intent here, because our concerns are centered directly on the fate of the 'potential' child, regarding our moral responsibilities toward that child. You know, the one who doesn't yet exist? We measure that unborn child's present state against its potential future state (which in my illustration is pretty much set in stone), and decide the obvious (if we're sane, anyway). Can anyone with a shred of human sensibility honestly say that nonexistence isn't preferable to the horrible life that awaits, should a potential parent decide to bring a new life into the kingdom of pain? It is in this sense that Benatar's third maxim, "the absence of pain is good, EVEN if that good is not enjoyed by anyone," holds true, and that it DOES hold true should be obvious to anyone guided by even the weakest empathic compass. The objection from 'non-identity' is revealed as a logomachian dodge.

Of course, the sadistic and brutal torture king doesn't actually exist on Earth, and never has. Not quite, anyway, though there have been several pretenders to the throne. So what are we talking here, in real world terms? Instead of the certainty of a dire ending for our children, reality presents us with a slightly more subtle dilemma. Chance. Possibilities. Hopes. But always, death.

Here's the deal, in the most straightforward metaphorical statement I can conceive at the moment. The seed is the cannonball. The womb is the cannon. The fuse is lit. The projectile is forcibly discharged into the air. In one sense, every firing is a risk. There are no guarantees that the projectile will reach its mark. Sometimes there are brick walls in the way that stop the ball from reaching its target. At other times, the trajectory is wrong, and the ball falls short. There are hundreds of other possible environmental factors that might influence the flight-path of the ball, and where it will ultimately land. Not to mention the inherent properties of the ball itself. All we know with practical confidence is that the ball WILL come to ground, somewhere, someday.

The differences between the cannonball and a human life are both numerous and obvious. The risk is the 'how,' and the 'where.' The certainty is in the sound of the 'splat.'

My younger daughter graduated from high school tonight. The ceremony was held outdoors, in the football stadium. I was sitting in the stands, reading over sections of *Better Never to Have Been* while waiting for the festivities to begin. I'd had to have been pretty dense not to appreciate the irony of the situation. Here was my daughter about to cross over this symbolic threshold into adulthood, while her father sat brooding in the grandstands contemplating her nonexistence. It seems callous, even to me.

Her plans are to go on to college, most likely majoring in music. She was her high school band's drum major for three years running. Played the trombone in both concert and jazz band. She even won awards for best overall musician, as well as best jazz musician. I'm very proud of her. I'm also scared to death. It's going to be a struggle getting through college, especially since her parents don't have the financial wherewithal to help her through the rough spots. I've never been much of a money machine. Claimed bankruptcy once several years ago. Since then, I've always existed close to the edge of insolvency. There won't be much assistance from this end when things get tight, I'm afraid.

Her older sister managed to plough through on her own for the most part. Working full-time. Commuting 45 miles back and forth to UC-Irvine. Another English major...ugh! (I'm just teasing about that, for if and when she ever reads this thing. I like to get my digs in). She's moved off to L.A. now. Landed a teaching job on the other side of the tracks, working with the sort of kids I've tried to keep her away from all her life. I worry about her. She's got a big dent in her self-confidence, exacerbated by some abandonment issues—owing in no small part to my waltzing off to Washington State to become the boy toy of a well-off woman I met on the internet, taking her little sister with me. Does she understand that I had no choice? And is what I just said the truth, or mere justification? Write me, and let me know.

Hey, it's not that I never saw her during the year and some months I lived in Spokane, shacking up with what turned out to be just another crazy bitch. As a matter of fact, she was up there with us when all the crazy shit went down. She was with me when we were forced to make a hasty departure in my overloaded GMC mini-pickup. California, here I come! Again. Since I'd pretty much decided that I'd be shooting myself in the head shortly after dropping the kids off at their mom's in Riverside, it seemed appropriate to take the long route south. Nothing like pre-suicide quality time with the kids.

We stopped in Medford, Oregon the first night. The town where I'd done my last four years of duty with the cult. Stayed with some old friends, then were off in the afternoon. We had to jog back north a few miles to catch the 99, then it was south across the border into California. Eventually we found ourselves on the 101 southbound, and smack in the middle of the biggest fucking trees any of us had seen in our lives. I'm talking about the mighty redwoods, of course, and fucking mighty do they be! I mean... *fuck!* Being in the midst of those grandfathers was off-the-charts awe-inspiring. The only thing I can compare it to is when the younger one and I took a boat 50 miles out into Lake Powell, to visit the majestic Rainbow Bridge in the middle of winter. We both sat down at the base of a ponderous limestone cliff-face nearby. Every few minutes we could hear the distant (and sometimes not-so-distant) sound of gigantic segments of rock peeling off and crashing into the ground below; the explosions echoed through the canyons, literally shaking the ground as we sat there, hyperventilating and eating our sandwiches. Playing chicken with a million-ton piece of the universe.

Jesus, am I a bad father, or what?

Anyway, the redwoods were kind of like that. Breathtaking. Scary. And really, *really* big! We even drove the truck through that one you see on all the postcards, the one with the tunnel carved through the middle.

After we got out of the tall trees, there really isn't much to tell. We had absolutely no money, so there was no question of lodging with real beds, or of hot and cold running water. The three of us slept in the little cab of my truck, huddled together like unbathed squirrels (not that I'd imagine squirrels bathe much). Our food consisted of what I could purchase on my Chevron card—frozen burritos, chips, Twinkies, and those crappy overpriced refrigerated sandwiches where the bread always tastes wet.

Two exceptions to this. Once, we found a station with a full Mexican kitchen behind the counter. Another time, there was an A&W attached to the Chevron, where they actually let me use my gas card. Hamburgers and root beer in frosted mugs that day, ladies and gentlemen!

And here's a point of interest. Did you know that, along pretty much the entire California coast, it's damned near impossible to set foot on the beach? Especially if you're poor. Where there aren't cliffs, there's private property. And where there's no private property, there are state beaches that charge admission. We did manage to skirt the rules now and again, trespassing to get our feet wet.

After seven days, including an excruciating stretch at the end, where it took us literally eight hours to get from Santa Monica to Riverside due to construction delays and Friday traffic, I dropped the kids off at their mom's, and commenced the contemplation of my doom. No, scratch that. First we detoured down to Murrieta and stayed with my mom in her apartment for a few days. THEN I dropped the kids off at their moms and went off to contemplate my doom. Points for accuracy.

The next few months were bad. I managed to hock a few things. A shotgun. A camera. A gold necklace I'd bought my wife for one of our happier anniversaries in the misty past. Maybe there was some other shit. I'm not sure. I lived on dollar hamburgers and chicken sandwiches from Carl's Jr. I spent most of the daytime hours in parks, cleaning up in the public restrooms, writing depressing poetry and multi-paged suicidal diatribes where I blamed everything and everyone but myself. I'd pitch my journal scraps into a trash can at the end of each day. It was summer and bejesus hot, and my feet and ankles swelled up due my uncontrolled high blood pressure to the point where all I could wear were unbuckled sandals. Sometimes I'd park under the mall parking structure and read old paperbacks until it got dark.

At night, I'd often pick up one or both of the kids and wheel over to the drive-in for a double feature. We'd usually stay for the second screening of the first movie, just so we could be together. Then I'd roll them home at 1 or 2 or 3 in the morning, parking up the street a ways from the house for a few hours of fitful, curbside sleep. It always made me paranoid sleeping out in the street in front of somebody's house. Some nights homeless hookers would rap on my window and order me to take them to the 24-hour McDonalds in exchange for favors. More often, I woke up with the sun, then drove over to join the early-rising retirees for a few miles of mall walking.

Sometimes I'd roll down to my mom's for a few days. That was nice. Showers. Television. Hot food. Company. But she lives on government assistance, and was always antsy about some bean counter auditing her one-tenant dwelling and kicking her out on account of my presence. Besides, I needed to be in Riverside to look for work, as it seemed apparent I didn't have the balls to swallow a slug for the cause. Thing is, though, it's hard to get motivated about job hunting when you have no address, no reliable place to clean up, no phone, no fax, no email address. Are those just excuses? Whatever. Fact is, I wasn't looking. I was becoming disturbingly resigned to an existence punctuated by rising and setting suns, and little more. Until one night.

I had discovered what I thought to be a relatively secure place to rest my head most nights (against the driver's side window). There was a mile-long street parallel to the 91 freeway, cut off from the lion's share of the traffic noise by a sound wall and set well away from the fronts of any homes with their nervous-Nellie occupants. It was a favorite parking place for neighborhood denizens running tractor-trailer rigs, and I'd taken to parking right behind one of those eighteen wheelers. Since the street was a rather extended section of unbroken straightaway, traffic tended to move along pretty fast. But there wasn't a lot of it, and it was generally quiet after midnight or so.

I think I settled in around 11 that night. I listened to the radio for a while, then swung my legs around and stretched them out as well as I could in the four-foot-wide cab of my pickup. I drifted in and out for a while, and had just entered into some now forgotten dream, when—BAM!

Well, not so much a *bam*, as a sort of slow motion lurch and crunch. The point of impact was right behind the door against which I was sleeping, with the intruding vehicle continuing its assault across the width of the door and into the front wheel-panel, stopping just inches short of the front left tire. I was pitched forward, striking my head against the cab's ceiling, and winding up with my face smashed flat against the passenger side window.

It took me a moment to get my bearings, then another few to realize what had happened. Long enough for the offender to have disappeared from the scene. I checked my watch: the stroke of midnight. Then came the cursing of God and country and pretty much everything else under the sun. Without even getting out to check the damage, I cranked up the engine and started driving. Amazingly, the impact, while being pretty severe, hadn't noticeably affected the truck's performance. The road I'd been parked on happened to dead-end at the mall. I squirted through the mostly deserted parking lot to the payphones over by the bus terminal and dialed 911. Since there was an actual police terminal at the mall, a squad car arrived in a couple minutes, and the officer took my information. After checking to make sure I had insurance (fortunately for me, it hadn't expired), he sent me on my way.

But I wasn't through. I was fucking pissed off, and I wanted revenge! Returning to the scene of the accident, I discovered a trail of liquid, and followed it down several streets into the heart of a condo community. Finally, along a section by and large unilluminated by the streetlights, sat the car that had hit me...deserted. The thing was an absolute wreck, despite the new car dealer plates. In the bad lighting, it appeared as if every square inch had been crunched, battered, or smashed. The hood was wide open, covering the broken windshield. Smoke poured from the engine, and coolant was hissing out the radiator. It reminded me of a murder victim lying in a pool of vital fluids.

While I was sitting there wondering what to do next, a couple of kids in another car rolled up. The passenger hopped out, leaned into what was left of the vehicle, and retrieved what appeared to be his wallet. He stopped and stared at me for a second, then hopped back into the other car and took off. But not before I managed to scribble down the license plate number.

Later on, I found out that the kid had stolen the car from his Mom's boyfriend. He had gone on a drunken rampage, totalling several other parked cars in the process. I guess I was lucky. My truck still ran fine, and the insurance settlement was enough for me to rent a room, providing me with a base of operations from which to get my life sort of back together again. However, that was a few weeks later, and not part of this story.

I stayed awake all the rest of that night, bleeding off the adrenaline. Just sitting there in my crumpled lifeboat, staring into the dark. Licking my wounds. School had started, and it was my habit to drive over to the ex's house early in the morning after she'd left for work and wait for the kids out in the driveway to give them a ride. That particular morning, they let me in the house to take a shower. A post-breakup breach of etiquette, I suppose. Then again, I'd relinquished pretty much everything to her in the divorce, so I figured fuck her. I needed that shower.

Naturally, she chose that morning to swing back around and check up on me (nosy neighbors with cell phones are not my friends). So she caught me in the house. Then she started chiding me. But I was in no mood to be fucked with that morning; and what with the previous night's adventure, not to mention the lack of sleep, I pretty much lost it and threw a fit. I even threatened to kill myself, if memory serves.

All this resulted in her calling the cops, who hauled me off to the mental ward for observation. It was an interesting five days. Nurses kept waving antidepressants under my nose on the hour. They all asked the same question. "Don't you want to get well?" I kept answering that I'd rather have some money, and a place to live. A psychiatrist with an eastern European accent kept telling me I was depressed and needed to take my meds. I told her I'd rather have some money, and a place to live. Some social welfare people interviewed me, dangling the hope for some money and a place to live under my nose for a few days, if only I would take my meds. Finally I took them, and didn't sleep for three days. So they took me off the meds. Then the social welfare people told me they couldn't do anything for me because I wasn't a drug addict. The very last thing any of them said to me was this: "So, they tell me you're living in your car. How's that working out for you?" It was then I understood why they only allowed me a two-inch wooden pencil.

Finally they sent me on my way with bare feet, and a bus pass.

So I sat in the football stadium tonight, and when they called my daughter's name I cheered, and laughed, and later I hugged her and told her how proud I was of her. My older daughter also graduated from college earlier this week, but none of us could afford the fees for the graduation exercises, so she didn't attend. I think she worked instead.

You never know what life's going to hand you. Things can be going along well for awhile, then BAM! Life can seem so full of promise sometimes, IF you're born into the right culture, in the right century, into a family with some means, and with a little luck. But even luck often fails you, sometimes drastically.

I wish my children well. I wish all children well. So what? When you get down to it, good intentions aren't worth squat. The best intentions do not in the least mitigate the harm we do, inevitably, to the children we create. We know our children will suffer and die. That makes all parents criminals in my book. Every last one of us.

F<small>INISHING UP AT NUMBER FOUR</small>, with a bullet:

> The absence of pleasure is NOT bad UNLESS there is somebody for whom this absence is a deprivation.

It looks like we're down to the fourth and final axiom of Professor David Benatar's existential quatrain. In the last section, I briefly discussed why the absence of pain is a good thing, stressing the self-evident nature of the statement from the standpoint of empathic awareness. Whether or not there exists an actual entity to appreciate that absence seems inconsequential. That the absence of pleasure is not bad to a non-existing sentient entity (or is it better to say "a sentient entity that doesn't exist?" Semantics!), seems logically to be the other side of the coin, and just as self-evident.

If you had the power to bequeath the sense of hunger to a rock, would you feel it important to do so, just so the rock might know how it feels to have its hunger sated? Whose purpose is being served here? Certainly not the rock's! Did the rock need any of this? Did it ask for it? And can you simply dismiss these concerns on the basis that, prior to your action, the rock didn't care one way or the other?

"But," you argue, "all my newly-invested-with-hunger rock wants to do is eat. Every time I offer it food, it grabs the morsel in its little rock mandibles, and swallows it down whole. I can plainly see the smile on its little rock face—proof that it enjoys eating. Furthermore, when I withhold food, it whines, and I can hear its tummy rumbling, and I can tell it's suffering discomfort. Isn't this proof that the rock values its hunger, making the sense of hunger valuable in and of itself?"

What you are describing is the state of a rock AFTER you've taken the liberty to change its nature, and not the nature of the original rock. Also, notice that in creating a sense of hunger in the rock, which is really an aspect of the sense of deprivation, you've also created the risk that sometimes the rock's hunger will go unsatisfied. Perhaps for extended periods of time, resulting in extreme suffering for the rock. The fact that the rock genuinely enjoys the pizza and toaster strudels you feed it, and in fact resents you terribly when you withhold them, only proves that the absence of pleasure is bad for a HUNGRY rock, and not for rocks in their natural, pre-hungry states.

And so it is with people. When we consider whether it is right to bring children into the world, we need to consider two questions:

1. What is better, from an empathic point of view? Suffering, or the absence of suffering? I ask the reader to consider this question in a general sense, in good faith, and not from the 'pain for gain' angle. For in truth, isn't the value of that kind of pain commensurate to the future suffering it helps us to avoid? As a matter of fact, pain is part of an elaborate biological avoidance system, ideally existing only as a means to an end, and not as an end itself. Unfortunately, we don't live on an ideal plane of existence. Pain becomes actualized, often hanging around far past its usefulness, and is replaced or combined with other pains, even creating new varieties of epiphenomenal suffering and distress, which are entirely detrimental, with absolutely no positive utilitarian underpinnings at all. This is the way of life. Suffering on top of suffering. No, not every moment. Nor

always unbearable, nor evenly distributed among the population. But the threat is always there, including the threat of the kind of inordinate suffering that decent people would never wish on anybody. The chance of ruination is always on the horizon. Thus we are cursed with running from the very thing that empowers our movement, compelled by the fear that things can (and very likely may, as we age) get worse.

2. What is worse? The absence of pleasure in an abstract being who will never feel deprived one iota of that pleasure? Or the experience of pleasure in an actual being, but a sense of pleasure which will always be mitigated to some degree by suffering, sometimes overshadowed to the point of obliteration? A transitory thing which must always remain partial at best, and which will disappear at the end as if it never were, from the standpoint of the one who has experienced it? How can we possibly label as 'bad' the absence of pleasure in someone who doesn't exist? If this is the case, then existence is actually worse than even the greatest pessimists dare imagine, for there are a literal infinity of abstract beings not experiencing pleasure right now! And that's a fact that can never be changed, no matter how many new lives we bring into the world.

This is the ludicrous state of affairs brought into play be denying Professor Benatar's fourth axiom.

It is often argued that life must be intrinsically good, since when questioned, most people respond that they're glad they were born. To put it another way, I think most people would agree that life's rewards are worth its slings and arrows. All part of the package, as it were. People assess the worth of pleasure against its experiential counterparts—pain, suffering and death—and for the most part, decide that life comes out on top, no matter the downside. But is this a realistic assessment, or is there some self-deception going on?

I was just reading about a famous Hollywood celebrity who recently deserted the ranks of Scientology. As a Scientologist, he made several declarations as to the efficacy of the organization's teachings, even investing his talents in promotional videos. Nowadays he considers all of it to have been a load of crap, and his fifteen-year membership to have been a total waste of time. I know the feeling. You invest yourself in a belief system, a program that speaks to your fears and desires. Soon you begin interpreting the world entirely along the lines of what you've been told. Counterevidence gets marginalized, nuanced out of existence, or simply discarded on the basis of its not being officially sanctioned information.

This kind of thinking isn't limited to the ranks of openly religious organizations. Humans have an unrivaled penchant for self-delusion, and for erecting structures to support those delusions. Lying to oneself is always easier when others are doing it along with you. A perfect example of this is outlined in the 1992 Frontline program *Prisoners of Silence*, a documentary exposing an ill-conceived teaching method for severely autistic children and young adults called 'facilitated communication.' With the help of a 'facilitator' guiding their hand over a keyboard, people with rudimentary to nonexistent communication skills were suddenly churning out sophisticated works of literature and poetry, including well enunciated diatribes against critics of the program. The movement flourished for years, until charges of sexual abuse against parents and caretakers began flaring up everywhere. Upon closer inspection through double-blind studies, it was ascertained, beyond any reasonable shadow of doubt, that the facilitators themselves were the ones inventing the abuse charges in the recesses of their own little subconscious fantasies. In fact, all the evidence pointed to the fact that the autistic subject was ALWAYS the unwitting proxy of the facilitator.

And yet, in the light of this discovery, the founders and practitioners continued to hold the banner of facilitated communication high. Many still do. Why? The motivations aren't too hard to ferret out. Emotional investment. Career investment. The wish to make a positive difference. What we want, what we wish to be, clouds our capacity for objective judgment. We harbor biases—biases that keep us from seeing the world as it truly is.

It is reasonable to ask: What role do our native biases play when it comes to judging our mortal predicament? After all, each of us is a microcosm of life itself. In being called to judge life in negative terms, aren't we really being asked to judge ourselves negatively? Who in hell wants to do that?

And so we learn to refract the atrocities of life through the prism of wish, to let our biases sift and filter and mold a preferred reality. In a literal and all-encompassing sense, this proves to be an impossible task. Life is just too filled with bad stuff to pretend it's not. Eschewing Pangloss, we simply shift the balance of our running equation; we learn to devalue the significance of certain data, while assigning undue value to other data. Such a tendency is supported by several factors—all basic survival instincts of various sorts. The natural disinclination to do one's self physical or psychical harm. The desire to support loved ones. Fear of death. All these, and many others I'm sure, feed into the culturally moored superstructure of self-delusion devised to tweak and distort our rational assessment of reality.

But deep inside. Oh yes, down in the emotional recesses, empathy is not being served. Empathy knows the score, and the best our survival-oriented valuations can do is offer up distractions. It's like letting the dog out on its leash so it doesn't tear up the yard.

Feed the starving nations, and ignore the fact that your benefaction ultimately, numerically worsens the problem.

Teach your children to concentrate on the positive. It's psychologically healthy, and they'll grow up wealthy and wise, to raise good little taxpayers.

Smile, and at least some of the world will smile with you. And you'll feel better, and so will they, and those positive feelings will help put the six o'clock news in proper perspective.

And so on.

L ET'S RECAP:

1. The presence of pain is bad.

Obviously.

2. The presence of pleasure is good.

Flipside.

3. The absence of pain is good, EVEN if that good is not enjoyed by anyone.

Bring me someone who experientially disagrees, then bring me a non-someone who experientially disagrees, and we'll talk. Otherwise, I'm sticking.

4. The absence of pleasure is NOT bad UNLESS there is somebody for whom this absence is a deprivation.

Again, bring me a non-entity, and I'll get the exclusive interview concerning his experiential state of deprivation.

It is unlikely that many people will take to heart the conclusion that coming into existence is always a harm. It is even less likely that many people will stop having children. By contrast, it is quite likely that my views either will be ignored or will be dismissed. As this response will account for a great deal of suffering between now and the demise of humanity, it cannot plausibly be thought of as philanthropic. That is not to say that it is motivated by any malice towards humans, but it does result from a self-deceptive indifference to the harm of coming into existence.

—David Benatar

It occurs to me that all of us are hanging from a ledge. We fight for room, jockeying for the best view. The safest spot. Calluses form on our fingertips as we move about the side of the building, seeking in desperation for an open window through which we might eventually escape our predicament. We keep reaching with our toes for a better purchase, being careful not to look down. Trying to forget about the pavement below, though we can't help but hear the occasional screams, and splats. After a while the muscles in our hands begin to weaken. Ligaments wither. Sometimes we can hear the cracking in the knuckles. Feel the tearing of the sinews. Our purchase becomes more and more precarious, but still we deny the drop that we know is coming. In a final, desperate bid of insanity to stave off the inevitable, we bite off little bits of flesh from our forearms and spit them up onto the top of the ledge we're grasping, somehow convincing ourselves that in this way the final descent won't be so painful, so terrifying. Then the moment comes. The fingers slip, one by one or all at once, and we plummet. Even on our way down, we fantasize that somehow, someone is waiting below to catch us. But there's never anybody there. Ever.

ESCAPE STRATEGIES

1. Life Looks Fine from Underneath the Bodhi Tree.

All Life is Suffering. This is the first tenet of Buddhism's 'Four Noble Truths.' It's also the only one of much consequence, as far as I'm concerned.

The story of the Buddha (enlightened one) is the tale of a young man named Siddhartha, which means 'the one whose wishes will be fulfilled.' Right off the bat I'd like to point out the fairytale-ish sense of the narrative, whereby the happy ending has already been back-engineered into the protagonist's name. Or title, which is probably more accurate. Thus the spoiler to the story's conclusion has already been supplied before any action has even taken place. Don't want people walking out of the theater (or monastery) in the middle of the show, do we?

Anyway, the story goes something like this.

Siddhartha was born in India, in a city called Kapilavatthu, somewhere in the foothills of the Himalayas. His dad was a rajah, his mom a queen. Making Siddhartha a prince, naturally. Two days after his birth, Siddhartha's mom dies unexpectedly (probably not THAT unexpectedly, the quality of post-natal care being what I assume it was in those days). Everybody's grief stricken, of course; no less the king, but he has other worries on his mind besides. Seems the court soothsayers have warned him that if Sid is ever exposed to sickness, old age, or death, the boy's gonna get a hankering to chuck off the royal accouterments and duties for a life of monastic asceticism. Seeking to forefend this unattractive prophecy, the king delegates the raising of his son to the court babysitter, and holds his breath.

Tradition's portrait of Siddhartha's formative years reveals a young man of exquisite sensitivity. Even though he was raised in an environment of loving kindness and opulence, on top of being extremely intelligent and popular amongst his peers, he was often distressed by the more inimical aspects of the natural world. For instance, he felt an extreme affinity with animals and would chastise others over their mistreatment. When his cruel cousin, Prince Devadatta, shot a swan with his bow and arrow (boys will be boys), Siddhartha nursed it back to health, then set it free. He also took notice of the inequalities of life. Once, at a ploughing festival, he watched with chagrin as his father drove a pair of bulls through the fields, using a whip. He couldn't help but note the incongruity between the obvious stress and pain the bulls endured as the happy and boisterous crowd cheered on their mistreatment.

There's also a story concerning Siddhartha's reflections on what nowadays (thanks to Disney) we've learned to exalt as the 'circle of life.' Lizard eats ants. Snake eats lizard. Bird eats snake. Etcetera. His observations made him realize that happiness is, at best, a transient thing—a temporarily gratifying sunbeam, doomed to be eclipsed by suffering. This realization disturbed Siddhartha profoundly. The knowledge that suffering exists at the very root of life came to haunt his every waking moment, overshadowing any sense of personal satisfaction despite his ostensibly rich and privileged lifestyle.

So the kid took to going off by himself into the woods, seeking escape in the silence of contemplation.

Naturally, his dad would have none of this. His worst fears were coming to fruition. To keep his son from leaving home, which could only serve to further hasten his disenchantment with the world, he arranged to have Siddhartha marry his own cousin (I know, but I don't think the ramifications were quite the same back then). They were both sixteen at the time (... again). The king granted them a pleasure palace in which to live, filled with singers and dancers and young, healthy specimens to keep the truths of suffering and death away from his oh-so-sensitive scion. An archetypal example of closing the barn door after the horse has escaped. True to form, and in spite of his father's best efforts, Siddhartha remained unimpressed, and glum.

Finally, at his son's insistence, the king granted Siddhartha a day pass into town, under supervision of his attendant, Channa. On his very first visit, he witnessed an old, frail man hobbling along amongst the passersby. Remarkably, owing to the machinations of his father, it appears that Siddhartha had managed to make it through most of his adolescence without ever having seen a human being of advanced age! Needless to say, our young prince did not sleep comfortably that night.

After he worked up enough courage to go out exploring again, Siddhartha ran across a man lying ill in the street. He went to help the guy, but Channa warned him off, explaining the nature of contagion, and the limits of Royal Immunity. Again, Siddhartha was nonplussed.

On their third visit, Siddhartha and Channa witnessed a funeral procession. At this point, the young prince had had enough. He returned to the palace that night determined to find a way to escape the harsh realities that he had seen.

One day shortly thereafter, while riding his horse in the garden, Siddhartha came upon a man adorned in simple yellow robes. The old gentleman seemed genuinely at peace with the world, happy and serene. It was explained to Siddhartha that this person was, in fact, an ascetic—a man who had walked away from everything in his life to find freedom from suffering. The idea appealed greatly to the prince, of course. Finally, when his dissatisfaction with the dancing girls, solid gold silverware, and custom woven mats for his chariot reached its peak (poor guy), Siddhartha slipped out of the palace, leaving his wife and newly born son behind. True to prophesy, he adopted the lifestyle of an indigent monk.

According to the stories, he spent the next several years practicing different forms of 'spiritual discipline' consisting of various approaches to meditation and contemplation, as well as the self-infliction of physical austerities. You know—starvation diets, sleeping on rocks, beating oneself in the face with a wiffle bat. That sort of thing. Unfortunately, none of this brought him any closer to his goal of release from suffering.

Well, that's not quite true; he almost starved himself to death, which would certainly have sufficed with respect to his immediate, personal concerns. But we have to consider the religious aegis under which Siddhartha was operating here. As a good Hindu boy, he would have been brought up believing in the karmic 'wheel o' debt,' whereby a soul is continually reincarnated to pay for the fuck-ups of the previous round. It's sort of like being in arrears to the Mafia, I guess; one never quite manages to get out from under. Realizing the futility of trying to get from point A to point B on a cosmic treadmill that never forgets, the wunderkind from Kapilavatthu finally chucked the disciplines, plopped his exceedingly bony ass down under the now legendary bodhi tree, and conjured up a more satisfactory, close-ended soteriology that would later be outlined in what came to be known as the 'Four Noble Truths.'

More satisfactory in assuaging his own personal demons, perhaps. For in truth, and after allowing for the axiomatic validity of the first precept, the Buddha's four-stage 'enlightenment' swiftly collapses into a rather self-centric coping mechanism. It's the original version of *I'm OK, You're OK*, a codified psychological gambit that would find successive expression in gnosticism, medieval post-Christian mysticism, Sufism, pantheism, and myriad esoteric systems. In more secular form, the same drill would later be rehearsed in the writings of the American transcendentalists, and later still in popular works by Aldous Huxley, Ram Dass ("Be Here Now"), Timothy Leary (in a silly sort of way), Stanislov Grof, Carlos Castaneda (in a REALLY silly sort of way), up to folks like Ken Wilbur and Echart Tolle ("Power of NOW"), and countless lecture circuit gurus. The common thread uniting these disparate traditions, movements and characters is, ironically, a connivance with an eye toward self-delusion reflected within the body of the Buddhistic doctrine itself.

So let's take a look.

1. ALL LIFE IS SUFFERING

Alternatively translated as 'life means suffering,' or 'there is suffering,' the word suffering being the closest English translation of the Sanskrit *dukkha*. Naturally there's been some quibbling over the exact meaning of the phrase; a tendency to try and soften the blow in these times when the more straightforward interpretation comes across as depressing and not really worthy of a demigod (in Nirvana, no one can hear you cry). But in the context of the chronicle I've briefly outlined, I think it takes a mighty disingenuous apologetic to evade the obvious implication of the phrase. There is pain. There is illness. There is fear. There is death. These are some of the aspects of life which denote suffering according to the most unambiguous usage of the word, and no minimally complex living creature escapes any of them.

As for those who would counter with the argument that, yes, suffering DOES exist, but only within a broader frame of reference which also includes the whole spectrum of experience, including great joy, the reader should note that this fact, while technically accurate, brought no solace to the young prince of Kapilavatthu. I don't doubt he acknowledged Creation's more agreeable charms. But in the face of transience and dissolution, such acknowledgement served merely to highlight the tragic absurdity of our existential plight.

If an apple has a small bruise, is the apple 'bad'? If it's limited to a small area, most people would say 'no.' They'd just cut away the bad piece, discard it, and eat the rest. But what if the bad spot is more substantial—say, 50% or so of the entire piece of fruit. Even so, it seems reasonable that half an apple is better than none at all, doesn't it? Still a lot of juicy Red Delicious there to be savored after the paring, isn't there? Of course, so far we're assuming the damage is isolated to one section of the apple, but as everybody knows, that's often not the way it works. In the case of our hypothetical apple, let's say the corruption has infiltrated the entire pulp. It remains true that—again, technically speaking—wholly 50% is still untouched, and highly edible. Unfortunately, it has become impossible to extricate the unspoiled parts from the permeating decay. Quibble over percentage points if you will, but at the end of the day, you're stuck holding a rotten apple.

"If I were to take the results of my philosophy as the standard of truth," wrote Arthur Schopenhauer, "I would have to consider Buddhism the finest of all religion."

Schopenhauer, who arguably lays claim to being the most explicitly pessimistic thinker in the history of modern Western philosophy, saw the rot too clearly. Parse away the metaphysical entanglements, lay aside the methodological ditch digging, and what you're left with are the bare bones of unadulterated rejection—a repudiation de force of the fundamental premise of existence itself.

The modern, street rendering of the primary Noble Truth? Life sucks, then you die.

2. THE CAUSE OF SUFFERING IS DESIRE

Desire is alternatively translated as 'attachment'; or, perhaps more pejoratively, 'craving.' I point this out because there's some not-so-subtle shading going on here. The word 'crave' holds a generally negative connotation, which serves to distance it by definitional degree from mere desire. After all, desire is endemic to the human condition, isn't it? We desire to eat, to breathe, to get out from under the rain, to copulate, to meditate, to sleep and to expectorate—*tra-la, tra-la, tra-la.*

As a matter of fact, the wish to be rid of desire is itself a desire. (This paradox, by the way, is a traditional koan used on Zen aspirants to get them to give up the desire to be rid of desire, which, about as often as not, just drives them nuts).

The point is that we want things, and we either don't get them, or we get them and lose them, or we get them, but the getting isn't nearly as satisfying as we thought it would be. We are unhealthily attached to things. To persons, to objects, to ideas—even to ourselves.

The grand upshot to all this (or the downfall, depending on one's degree of 'attachment') is that everything we desire, or feel, or experience—in other words, the totality of our experiential lives—is, in reality, ephemeral, illusory bullshit. Our desires can never be truly fulfilled for the simple reason that nothing really exists! Nothing exists of itself. There is no truly objective autonomy anywhere in the universe—subject, object, or thought. Like Whitehead said, "It's all just process, man!"

Or, maybe Tull said it better:

How does it feel to be in the play?
How does it feel to play the play?
How does it feel to BE the play?

To put it another way with special reference to suffering, it is often said in mystic circles, 'there is no sufferer, only the suffering.' According to this view (and a solid scientific case can be made for this view, by the way), nothing exists apart from the whole, but because we don't realize this 'oneness' of all things, we suffer. Or more accurately, 'suffering exists.' Unfortunately, such a meta-perspective as this is about as far removed from everyday experience as one can get. How does one achieve such an exalted outlook, especially considering the fact that there's nobody around to benefit from such an achievement in the first place? More importantly, what is the real value of seeing things this way in terms of the planetary aggregate of human experience?

In my opinion, there is none. Or at least, very little. Others would beg to differ.

3. THE CESSATION OF SUFFERING CAN BE ATTAINED

And how is that to be accomplished? It logically follows that if, indeed, desire is the cause of suffering, then through the extinguishment of desire suffering will vanish. The third Noble Truth is embodied in the term *nirodha*—a Hindu expression meaning a state of mental concentration in which the experiential distinction between subject and object is destroyed, so that the mind attains realization of non-duality. Or, in abbreviated Buddhistic form, *nirodha* is simply the cessation of *dukkha*. And what is *dukkha*, you ask? (You DID ask, didn't you?). While there's no precise English equivalent, *dukkha* is usually translated as unhappiness, unsatisfactory conditions, the sense of futility, despair, anxiety, illness, anomie, transience; or, to wrap it all up in a neat (and by this point in the book, familiar) little descriptor: *suffering*.

So the third Noble Truth's claim boils down to this. The elimination of suffering is possible, but only through the eradication of desire. In fact, the ultimate goal of Buddhistic thought and praxis is nothing more nor less than achieving a thoroughly detached attitude towards the flux of existence. Easy come, easy go. Through detachment, utter serenity is achieved (along with the usual superstitious, metaphysical baggage that comes along with practically any religious belief system—in this case, release from karmic death and literal absorption into the Eastern iconography of the Supreme Godhead).

I probably should state up front that I have no real problems with any of this. At least, not from the personal improvement angle. Hey, whatever floats your boat is fine with me, and I'll admit there's a lot to be said for this approach in the arena of psychological health. But let's say for a moment that somebody actually reaches that Nirvanic paradise, and is even now waving back at us from that other shore, considering all us poor heathens mired in this pit of *samsara* (the cycle of birth, suffering, and death in the material world) with the cool eye of utterly composed detachment. My question is this: What the hell good does that do for anybody else? It's all fine and dandy to point out the illusory nature of the illusory fire burning down the illusory orphanage, but what about all that goddamned screaming?

Oh, yeah...illusory, right?

Well, fuck that. I don't *want* to see things that way.

Even if I could.

Of course, adherents will insist that such dispassionate 'enlightenment' actually increases compassion. I'm in no position to dispute that point. I'll even acknowledge that a lot of negative human behavior probably stems from unhealthy psychological fixations. But so what? Against the greater scheme of worldly suffering, you have a select few cloistered mystics, sequestered away from the realities of life, contemplating their bellybuttons in bubbles of rarefied enlightenment. What difference does it make to those sitting ringside, or to those being pummeled in the ring? To those for whom escape was never an option?

Then again, I suppose it's a boon for the manufacturers of those little plastic Buddha bottles filled with cheap aftershave that I used to get for Christmas. Whatever happened to those little guys, anyway?

4. THERE IS A PATH TO THE CESSATION OF SUFFERING

Specifically, an 'eightfold' path, comprised of eight aspects designed to loosen desire's hold on us. Meant as both a practical approach to living in the world, as well as a mental discipline, they are:

1. Right View
2. Right Intention
3. Right Speech
4. Right Action
5. Right Livelihood
6. Right Effort
7. Right Mindfulness
8. Right Concentration

I have no intention of delving into vicissitudes. Suffice it to say that it's all just another gimmick to make people feel better about their circumstances by learning to not actually care about what circumstances they're stuck in. That's not to say it's a *bad* gimmick. There's nothing really that terrible about learning to accept the inevitable, I suppose. No doubt a lot of anxiety churns up when biologically-centered self-defense mechanisms tangle up with the abstract worlds we all carry around in our heads. When we're barraged by credit card offers, bill collectors, pink slips, and the knowledge of our imminent death, all the adrenaline overflow in the world fails to serve much practical purpose. In the long run, it results in hypertension, heart problems, dog kicking, spousal abuse, and general crankiness.

Eastern thought tends to generate Eastern platitudes, turning subjective psychological states into objective statements about reality that are just so much horseshit. This tendency is especially pernicious amongst Western adherents, who can't resist putting a 'can do' spin on fashionably exotic concepts. It's one thing to learn to arrest or ignore one's feelings of hunger. It's quite another to say others are hungry only because they've not learned to quench their desires in the Eternal Now. Yet, this IS the goal, as if seeing things a different way actually changes the way things are. "Changing the world from within." "The world is perfect just the way it is." Or the old standby, "Life is good." The truth of such statements survives only insofar as objectivity is thrown out the window in exchange for a fallaciously crafted peace of mind.

How can anyone consider the history of the human race and make a statement like "Life is good"? Only a person who has learned to thoroughly deceive himself could make such a claim. And while such self-deception is a raw universal trait within the species, Oriental thought, along with its New Age offshoots, have turned it into an art form.

Poor Siddhartha. To see such ugliness in the midst of opulence. I feel for the guy. I also totally empathize with his need to escape, to find a refuge from the encroaching horror, even if it ultimately wound up being a philosophical delusion. You know, there have been some very hard times down through history. Times of famine, when parents ate their children believing they were bread. Sometimes madness fills the belly. Sometimes lies provide solace. Most of the time, now that I think about it.

nature's a killer I won't sing to it
I hold my breath and listen to the dead singing under the grass
      —Ikkyu Sojun

2. In Heaven, No One Can Hear You Scream.

Ah, wacky, wonderful theism! Ten thousand sects, each with their variant stabs at origin and purpose! As well as those frightful eschatologies screen-tested to keep trembling widows up at night, hoping and praying that their messiah is the RIGHT messiah! I'll try to confine my remarks to the prevalent religious belief system of the Western world, Judeo-Christianity, since it pretty much covers what I'd say about Judaism by itself. Besides, I have little knowledge of (and even less interest in) the Jihad-happy madness of the Mohammedans. Inner struggle, my ass.

By now, the reader will have caught a piquant whiff of my general disdain for Christianity. I guess the part that bugs me the most is that, here we are, denizens of the 21st century, grandchildren of the Enlightenment, still held hostage by a bunch of primitive yokels burning incense to a tyrannical sky wizard. Offering up our children via catechisms and holy wars to a deity who thinks we're all shit. My ex-wife is one of them and when she tells me she's in love with a God Who will most likely one day cast her unbelieving daughters and once-beloved husband into the eternal Lake of Fire... well, sometimes a small part of me wants to knock her teeth right down her throat. But I digress.

Still, with all her faults, I have to give the Church *some* credit. For all the goofy ritual and phantasmagorical allegory (what was that John of Patmos smoking, anyway?), the writers and subsequent adherents of the New Testament have got one thing indisputably correct. In fact, considering both the internal and external inconsistencies, not to mention the downright primitive ludicrousness of this collection of redacted gospels and Pauline epistles (half of which are probable forgeries), there is one solid, unbroken theme that runs throughout. In fact, if I had it my way the title page would look something like this:

The New Testament
Or: Life Sucks and Then You Die

The motif actually starts near the very beginning of the book of Genesis, in the so-called Old Testament. People aren't in the utopian garden for a week before they fuck things up, eating poison fruit from some evil tree which, for some reason, God didn't have enough foresight to protect them from. Or, maybe He hadn't invented cyclone fencing yet. Anyway, the formerly immortal Adam and Eve are unceremoniously booted out of paradise, and cursed with mortality (although I guess 900+ years isn't bad compared to today's three score and ten). As are all their descendents, including...well, everybody! Deific grudges, it would seem, are the worst kind.

The rest of the O.T. is an accounting of one ancient nation's attempt at making things right with their Creator. This shouldn't have been that difficult from a moralistic perspective, considering what a Giant Prick their Creator turns out to be. It was probably tough getting an accurate read on just what might please the Almighty Despot in the Sky. How do you predict the moods of One Who turns a blind eye to rape, pillaging, slavery and even genocide (fact is, He often commanded such atrocities), then whips right around and has you executed for picking up sticks on Saturday? To say that God's ways are mysterious is a mordacious understatement.

The basic message behind all this is, of course, that life is fucked-up, and there's really not much of anything you can do about it. Oh, there are the blood sacrifices; but really, you might as well apply a bandage to a gangrenous wound. The rot is in the meat, as it were. Do your best, make sure the menstruating females are sequestered outside the presence of decent folk, don't mix your fabrics, and know that anything you do will never be quite good enough to make things right.

To give the ancient Israelites some credit, at least there was no afterlife to worry about, and no furnace room packed with infernal torture devices designed to make the chosen few that much more grateful (better them than us). The concept of life after death came along with the Persian captivity... or was it the Babylonian? Come to think of it, for the Chosen People of the biggest goddamned God this corner of the galaxy, ancient Israel sure got pushed around a lot. Maybe that's the natural course of events for xenophobic nations whose God's bark is worse than His bite. Looking at the state of the Mideast today, I'd say the rule still holds.

Eventually, Jesus came along. Born of a virgin, by most accounts. Born of a hodgepodge of competing mythologies, according to authentic historians. The way the story's interpreted these days, God got sick up to here with burnt goat, so He cut off His own arm and sent it down to earth in human form in order to magically turn some water into wine, ride a donkey, get nailed to a cross, walk around as a zombie for a while, then return to Heaven to sit on its own throne and eventually judge and condemn all Hindus, Buddhists, Unitarians, Mormons, gypsies, Shriners, homos and chimpanzees who use sign language, consigning them to the fiery pits of His Dad's basement.

Something like that.

OK, then. Christianity's metaphysical take on reality is somewhat...fanciful? Weird? Bat-shit crazy? All granted. Yet there is one sentiment expressed throughout the Bible that I share with utter certitude, and that is this: Life is not what it should be. Oh, not in the sense that it doesn't line up with some all powerful Monarch's Prime Directive. We've already been over all that Kantian imperative bullshit. But taken as a metaphorical statement, the personification through narrative of a fallen mankind is really the story of how we see ourselves—of how we *relate* to each other, to the earth, and to the universe. At every turn, we fall short of our own ideals. We try to justify our existence by sundry means. By good works, by sacrifice, even by self-effacement and humiliation.

Ancient blood sacrifice failed on two fronts. Obviously, as a bribe to the Celestial Referee it was absolutely worthless. In fact, it was genuinely counter-productive, in that the Israelites were forced to blame themselves time and again for its utter lack of efficacy. God always gets the credit, never the blame. Furthermore, the very act of animal murder served as a sublimated reminder of how fucked-up the whole scheme of things really is. Why do you think the more pacifistic religious and political movements stress vegetarianism?

In a sense, the Jesus mythology represents a transcendental endgame. One final sacrifice, big and bold! In fact, it is the Deity sacrificing Itself to Itself. Surely this MUST be enough to balance the books! The final recompense to lift the stain and make all things pure. As a matter of fact, the Jesus of the gospels believed that His Presence was the immanent trigger meant to usher in a whole new world free of both pain and death, forever and ever, amen. Never mind that things didn't actually work out that way. Through creative exegeses and pious fraud, subsequent generations of the faithful have turned the literal, real-world interpretation of the gospel event into a psychological redoubt from which to see the world as they'd like to see it.

And how do they see the world? As a grimy, out-of-the-way bus stop in Shithole, New Mexico. As a temporary inconvenience, like waiting in line at the DMV for those shiny new, personalized license plates. Christians are ready to get the hell OUT of here, man! On with the afterlife! Why do you think some of the most popular Christian authors are those who expound, in lurid detail, on all that dreary end-times stuff? Apocalypticism sells. Blow up the world, we want to get off! However...

Now things get a bit complicated. First of all, Christians are stuck here. At least for now. Regenerate saints living among the unwashed. For most, suicide isn't an option; that is, unless one manages to get oneself trampled to death during an anti-abortion rally (in Jesus' name, of course). And despite the mess people have made of it, it's still God's world. There's still a harvest of souls to be reaped, you know? And here's where the first notes of theological schizophrenia come into play. Doesn't logic dictate that, in a world where all have fallen and most will never get up, we should cease and desist in this haphazard manufacturing of souls? Hell may indeed be the chthonic equivalent to Hilbert's grand hotel of infinite rooms, but if we continue filling them, what becomes of Kingdom Come?

Ah, but then there's that OTHER Godly maxim to be dealt with: "Be fruitful and multiply, and fill the earth"—Genesis 1:28. What to do, what to do? But the anonymous author of the second epistle of Peter had an answer. Here are the high points, with commentary:

> *3:1 This second epistle, beloved, I now write unto you; in both which I stir up your pure minds by way of remembrance:*

> *3:2 That ye may be mindful of the words which were spoken before by the holy prophets, and of the commandment of us the apostles of the Lord and Saviour:*
>
> *3:3 Knowing this first, that there shall come in the last days scoffers, walking after their own lusts,*
>
> *3:4 And saying, Where is the promise of his coming? for since the fathers fell asleep, all things continue as they were from the beginning of the creation.*

In other words, where the hell is Jesus? He's late! People are getting sick and old and dying, yet nothing's changed.

> *3:5 For this they willingly are ignorant of, that by the word of God the heavens were of old, and the earth standing out of the water and in the water:*
>
> *3:6 Whereby the world that then was, being overflowed with water, perished:*
>
> *3:7 But the heavens and the earth, which are now, by the same word are kept in store, reserved unto fire against the day of judgment and perdition of ungodly men.*

He's coming already! He's a busy man, what with the managing of every subatomic particle in the universe! Oy! Be patient, or when He gets here He's gonna give you so much shit!

> *3:8 But, beloved, be not ignorant of this one thing, that one day is with the Lord as a thousand years, and a thousand years as one day.*

Remember the 'Church Lady'? "How con-veeeeenient!"

> *3:9 The Lord is not slack concerning his promise, as some men count slackness; but is longsuffering to us-ward, not*

willing that any should perish, but that all should come to repentance.

And since He hasn't deigned to provide us with birth control devices yet, we can count on His suffering for a long time to come.

3:10 But the day of the Lord will come as a thief in the night; in the which the heavens shall pass away with a great noise, and the elements shall melt with fervent heat, the earth also and the works that are therein shall be burned up.

3:11 Seeing then that all these things shall be dissolved, what manner of persons ought ye to be in all holy conversation and godliness,

3:12 Looking for and hasting unto the coming of the day of God, wherein the heavens being on fire shall be dissolved, and the elements shall melt with fervent heat?

3:13 Nevertheless we, according to his promise, look for new heavens and a new earth, wherein dwelleth righteousness.

Keep looking to the sky! The fireworks are sure to commence...someday? During the interim, feel free to copulate like bunnies.

In a nutshell, this delayed eschatological strategy allows Armageddon-minded Christians to live in a sort of sliding state of denial, all the while maintaining the status quo. They can live in a bubble of future promises overlaid on present circumstances. To ratchet up the cognitive dissonance, they've been given the Holy Spirit, or indwelling presence of the Deity, through Whose eyes they can project the future New Earth onto the old one, no matter how nasty the present situation might actually be.

But that's now. What about THEN, after the four horsemen and the avenging angels, when the moon's been bled dry and the stars have fallen? Heaven, right? The final judgment. The separating of the sheep from the goats before the BIG everlasting party starts. And who are the goats? Well, according to this, most of us:

> *Enter ye in at the strait gate: for wide [is] the gate, and broad [is] the way, that leadeth to destruction, and many there be which go in thereat: Because strait [is] the gate, and narrow [is] the way, which leadeth unto life, and few there be that find it." Matthew 7:13-14*

You know what that means, don't you? Eternal damnation. Torture of the mind (and perhaps the body, though there's the question of what kind of body that might be) for all of endless time. Suffering on a scale that makes all the atrocities anyone's ever been subjected to here on earth added up together seem like a pleasant massage. And with absolutely no hope of diminishment, much less surcease.

And who will make up this gaggle of victims? Drive out to the nearest mall on a Saturday, grab yourself a squishee at the food court, and take a good look around. Husbands, wives, fathers, mothers, babies... as well as the kid who just served you that soft pretzel, the one who's not making great grades, but still dreams of being a dental hygienist. Oh, let's be generous and round it out to eight out of ten of everyone you see. All going to hell. Forever.

Then again, maybe you don't need to drive downtown after all. Just look into the eyes of your own children, and imagine one of them coming in the house one day and announcing, "Mom. Dad. I am now a Unitarian." That'll be a milk-through-the-nose moment, eh?

Face it. The whole heaven/hell thing is predicated on the idea that each of us has free will, and that most of us will choose the path that "leadeth to destruction." This isn't my reality, but if it's yours, shouldn't any thought toward bearing children take account of these most ultimately horrible of stakes? Think about it. Hold nonexistence in your right hand, and an eternity of unbearable agony, which must nonetheless somehow be borne, in your left. Is there ANY question as to the more favorable state you'd want your child to end up in, after his body has gone to ground?

Now, after allowing the utter obviousness of my rhetorical question to sink in, consider this. The right hand path, or the state of nonexistence, is exactly the state that a Christian yanks his child *out of* in the first place. And according to Matthew 7:13-14, the odds of that child's damnation to a place of everlasting torment are AT LEAST as good as playing Russian Roulette with five bullets in the chamber.

That's, uh...not good.

3. Tomorrow's promise.

How's that song from *Annie* go? "The sun'll come up... somethin, somethin?" Yeah, it probably will come up tomorrow, barring some fluky astrophysical occurrence that throws the balance between the sun's thermal and gravitational pressures out of their present state of relative equilibrium. But what kind of world will tomorrow's sun look down upon? How many life forms will wither under its indifferent countenance? Oh, and let's not forget skin cancer!

Obviously, Annie isn't singing about the literal sun. The coming of tomorrow's sun is a metaphor for hope. It's kind of a promise that, no matter how bad one's present circumstances, things can (and by "can," she means a heavily implied "will") get better. Tomorrow. Or in the near future, anyway. You know, blue skies are gonna clear up, so put on that happy yada, yada, yada. It's always darkest before the dawn. Even though your heart is breaking; laugh, clown, laugh!

Our culture is bloated with such expressions. Hope sells. Why? Because people want things to be better than they are. And why's that? Well, it logically follows that if people are looking toward the future, the present isn't quite as good as the future of their imaginations, which is to say, the way things SHOULD BE. Not according to a mandate from Heaven (we just got done exploring that avenue), but according to how people gauge their own happiness, which is also usually tied in to the existential state of their loved ones, friends, and neighbors. Everybody wants things to get better somehow, someday. And it's axiomatic that if we want a 'better' future, the present falls into the category of 'worse.'

Many of the sciences are concerned with the problem of how to make life better. Medicine in particular seeks to ease us through this short excursion from cradle to grave, while at the same time extending the number of years it takes to get there. Medical practitioners have learned a lot about what keeps a body ticking. They have devised oodles of neat tricks to stave off infirmity and dissolution. Hell, they've been replacing organs since 1954, the year before I was born! Now they're doing fingers and toes and arms and legs, and even hair, for crissakes! The future is here, my friends! The future is now.

Naw! The future is neither here, nor now. What will be, soon becomes what is. Which, before you know it, passes irrevocably into what was. How can this be? Did we miss something? We arise to a morning sun filled with promise, but forget about all that shit before breakfast. By noon we're complaining about the heat. Come sunset, we pull the drapes and start knocking back brewskis. We watch imaginary characters leading imaginary lives on television. Just before bedtime, we check the news to be sure we're up on our tally of dead and wounded, and we don't even notice it's gotten dark outside again. But if we're halfway pious, right before we go to bed we pray that the sun'll come up...tomorrow.

Betch'er bottom dollar.

Nonetheless, some day things really WILL get better. How do we know this? Why, because it's something we want to happen, right? And surely everybody knows that the universe is arranged for our ultimate benefit. Right? Our predecessors' lives may have been mere fodder. But the work of their hands and minds, as well as their rotting bodies, will serve as mulch for the future Utopian Garden of Earthly Delights.

Or perhaps I'm being a little premature there. It may very well be that we'll slough off these meat-pies we call bodies, and depart this region of the galaxy before we finally get our cumulative acts together. But get them together we shall, whether we wind up as gas clouds, or floating balls of light, or something resembling the Borg (plural) of *Star Trek TNG*.

Or perhaps we'll live computer generated and enhanced virtual lives, where reality will be any damned thing we want it to be. Virtual meeting places will be peopled with a thousand variations of Fabio and Angelina. Legions of unfuckable nerds will rejoice as our pasty little bodies are honeycombed underground somewhere like in *The Matrix*, sustained by automatic, self-repairing nano-apparati. I suppose even then there might be an upper limit to bodily longevity. But we'll probably learn to squeeze years, or even centuries, into virtual seconds by then. Not categorical immortality, perhaps, but we'll make Methuselah look like a mayfly.

These and other imaginative future scenarios emerge from the minds of that loose-knit body of freaks and geeks which I shall henceforth label as 'futurists.' The web is crawling with these guys (curiously, not so many female voices). By and large, futurists are inordinately bright, optimistic visionaries. They have an eye toward extending human longevity, while at the same time enhancing the overall human experience. A few of those I've read (between the lines) seem to be primarily motivated by an unbounded fear of death, clutching at the straws of hope that mankind will achieve Utopia before it's too late to do them any good. There's one particular fellow who's so scared shitless of shucking off his mortal overcoat that he actually advocates any horrendous human experimentation imaginable in the dim hope that it might serve to move society half a notch further towards prolonging life. He even stated once that he would rather endure an eternity of hellish torture than die. I suspect this is either a young guy who's led a rather charmed life, or maybe he just hasn't thought things through. Either way, I hope he never becomes a physician.

But aside from those few with arguably sociopathic leanings (you'll find one or two in every bunch), I generally admire what motivates these guys. They're not stupid. Most of them know the breakthrough advancements in life extension they're hoping for are still some distance over the bio-technological horizon. Probably too far off to do them much good. No, this is a multi-generational problem, extending into a future we can only glimpse by dint of sustained optimistic hypothesizing. The futurists' hope rests not in those of us who live now. This is about the survival of the species, those abstract legions of people yet to be, who MUST someday be. Because... because...

Well? Why MUST they be? That's the question far too few of these guys ask themselves. Why is it so important to fill up every future moment with people? Before the first hominid stood up to get a better look over the savannah, was there something fundamentally missing in the universe? If tonight we all went to bed and just didn't wake up, what difference would it make? We are temporal creatures living on a speck of dust in a microscopic corner of one of hundreds of billions of galaxies. What is so crucial about our particular existence that we feel compelled to roll children out of their eternal slumber, slap them around for awhile, feed them, fuck them, pull them through knotholes, blindfold them, turn them round and round, then send them back off to find their beds? It makes no sense!

Unless, of course, we don't want to die, and are willing to do ANYTHING to avoid it. And by anything, I mean conjuring up imaginary selves who somehow survive the death of the body, and continue on into the hypothetical future, piggybacking on the abstract lives of people who don't yet exist. To further complicate things, and due to the fact that we know damned well the next generations will ALSO suffer and die, our vicarious selves are forced to generation-hop, again and again, in order to avoid extinction. An extinction, by the way, which is only avoided in terms of imaginative fancy, and never in reality.

Now that I think about it, it all sounds a lot like a pyramid scheme, doesn't it?

Sigh. There he goes with that vicarious immortality shit again. OK, I'll admit I've probably beaten that plow horse into glue, but...well, it's kind of important to me that everybody's clear about what's going on here. The reasons we have children are ALL selfish ones. These are of three types:

1. *'Feelings' motivated selfishness*, i.e., the warm fuzzies and/or the chest-beating ego trip. Look what I did!

2. *Utilitarian selfishness*, by which we view our progeny as ultimately 'useful' in some more or less direct sense, whether as family providers, soldiers, taxpayers, voters, or caregivers.

3. *Self-deluded selfishness*, whereby we seek to obtain immortality by vicarious means, through the continued survival of the species.

Here are some synonyms I found during a word study of 'vicarious':

feigned, counterfeit, assumed, affected, shammed, bluffing, simulated, dissimulated, lying, falsified, put on, concealed, covered, masked, cheating; see also false, fake, make-believe, mock, nominal, unreliable.

In other words, vicarious immortality is FAKE immortality. It doesn't exist outside the human imagination. I may be in danger of belaboring a point here, but before the reader is tempted to protest my several iterations as a mere display of condescending pedantry, consider what the simple contemplation of mass human extinction elicits in people. The answer, for those playing along at home, is HORROR.

Now consider that most of us, futurists notwithstanding, have come to an uneasy acceptance of individual mortality. Like it or not, all of us are eventually touched by death through the loss of friends, neighbors and loved ones. But what's the universal response in such instances?

"Life goes on."

How many times have we heard this, or said it ourselves—though ofttimes in the stoic manner of an uttered curse? Even for those of us who believe in only subjective annihilation after death, this unadorned avowal seems to convey the sense of an existential umbilical cord extending from the center of our apparent individual mortality and carried along through subsequent generations into the distant, hazy future where certainly "all shall be well, and all shall be well, and all manner of thing shall be well." Not so curiously, this famous quotation comes from a 14th century Catholic mystic, Julian of Norwich, who wrote of the Holy Trinity in domestic terms, speaking metaphorically of Jesus as a mother in connection with procreation and upbringing. Figures. It's a very motherly lie, isn't it? "Oh, don't bother yourselves over that Black Plague, dearies! Do your lessons, say your prayers, and everything will be fine...tomorrow. Life goes on, you know!"

But enough about motivations and the lies sustaining them. There are other questions. For instance: beyond the fact that the futurist's enthusiastic vision is built on a scaffolding of bones and heartache, what guarantees have we that our successors will ever reach that other shore? Where's the historical precedent that such idealism is grounded in anything other than pure fantasy? Haven't we been here before? Thus far, utopian architects have only managed to achieve the rather dubious distinction of *getting it wrong every time*. What's the justification for believing things will ever be different, beyond what I suspect is a teleologically salted superstition that some invisible force, something akin to an animated Platonic idealism, perhaps, is really running the show? Shades of Telliard de Chardin, Batman! Show me the money!

Beyond the question of whether such idealism is achievable (it's not), there's also the problem of *sustainability*. Once we bring about The Singularity, or Oneness, or Universal Harmony, or whatever it is we think we want, how can we be sure it won't be mucked up in a month? If there's anything predictable about human beings, it's that we're unpredictable. Isn't the story of the Devil's revolution in Heaven really just a metaphor for the fact that you can't make everybody happy all the time? Maybe happiness is at least partly based upon change, and even conflict. Trouble is, in pretty much any conflict, there are winners. And there are losers. Poof! There goes another Paradise.

There's still one problem I haven't addressed, which is by far the most potentially terrifying. Many, if not most, of the futurists' aspirations lie in the manipulation of human consciousness. I already mentioned the 'virtual reality' aspect. Most of us are aware of this concept as it was popularized in *The Matrix*, but there's also talk of drastic mood enhancement, either through drugs or some kind of direct computer interface juicing up our happiness receptors. "Imagine," the would-be post-human says, "the best orgasm you ever had, TIMES A THOUSAND!"

There are a few presumptions operating here that I'm not ready to buy into. Beyond what I think might be a rather naive confidence in the science involved, I'm wondering if everybody will be amenable to such a master plan. At any given moment, there are a million agendas in the world, and a lot of them have to do with power. And there are those pesky gods to deal with. Futurists are secularists, generally speaking, and secularists are still a minority in this world, barely tolerated by those who derive their power from the god-fearing masses. Ironically, it requires an act of faith to believe that any major change in such a state of affairs is even remotely foreseeable.

Next, there are questions having to do with the nature of happiness itself. I'm not so sure happiness is some latent birthday balloon lying just under the surface of our psychic sea, appearing now and again according to the whims of waves and weather, but ready to inflate and dominate with the utilization of a little fortified laughing gas. I tend to see the whole emotional matrix as the end product of evolutionary adaptation. A bundle of response mechanisms that owe their existence, at least to some degree, to the relative interplay between the various parts. In this respect, perhaps 'ultimate happiness' makes no more sense than 'ultimate upness,' where peaks of bliss can only be said to exist in relation to the slopes, drops, and valleys of the entire emotional mountain range. If this is true (and I've seen no evidence to the contrary), happiness may to some degree depend on the contrast of its opposites to keep everything from sliding into a self-destructive ennui, or something worse. Who knows?

But the part about all this that scares me the most, is the part where the fundamental control of people's sentience falls into the wrong hands. Imagine a malignant personality or organization with unrestricted access to your very soul, dear reader. Your mind a playground for the most gross perversions imaginable—indeed, *beyond* what is imaginable. Heinous torments drawn out for decades, yet so compressed in time that each hour might be made to correspond with a subjective millennium. Suffering completely off the scale of present-day human experience, and your only hope for surcease manufactured by your torturers as something to be intermittently raised and quashed, used only as a tool to further intensify the quality of your pain. A literal hell on earth, embedded in the code. To be downloaded and traded and copied in perpetuity as a matter of caprice.

Now ask yourself this: somewhere along the timeline of this hypothesized future—and I would argue here that my conjectural scenario is at least as valid as the more optimistic ones floating around out there—mightn't you reach a point where you wished you'd never been born?

Of course, none of us living is likely to experience such a future. At least, I hope not. But some day, somebody probably will. Maybe a lot of people. That is, of course, unless nobody's left around.

That is my hope for tomorrow.

FAUX
Q & A

If you were to ask people the question "are you glad you were born?," can you honestly doubt that most would answer in the affirmative? Accepting for the sake of argument that this is true, doesn't this sole fact undermine your whole premise that life is ultimately not a worthwhile endeavor?

I'll concede that, when asked the question in this way, most people would say they're glad to be alive. Not everyone, mind you. And not without qualification. I'm reminded of a fly-by conversation I had with a homeless woman out in front of the 99cent store one morning. We started talking about life, and how hard it is to get by sometimes. At some point during our chat, she remarked, "You know, I wouldn't even care if it wasn't for my kids. I'd just as soon have it over with." The temptation for many armchair health professionals would be to diagnose this woman's attitude in terms of clinical depression, no doubt brought on by conditions related to poverty. Or conversely, perhaps her indigence was a direct result of clinical depression, making it impossible for her to get her act together. Notice that either way her perspective can be isolated, minimized, and finally disregarded as statistically irrelevant in the face of the general, 'happy' population. When happiness is the definitional norm, all contrary minority attitudes can be categorized as aberrant.

I see I've gotten ahead of myself, accepting as a given that "I'm glad to be alive" equates to 'happiness.' But isn't that what we all assume? Or if not happiness, at least some degree of release from unhappiness? Honestly, I'm not even sure how to parse the difference. What are we seeking when we try to allay unhappiness, if not happiness? Neutrality?

I think the real question here is whether or not the general level of happiness supports this 'glad to be here' feeling that almost everybody purportedly claims to have. Take work. How many people do you know who are truly happy with their jobs? If the number is very large, you are either one of the fortunate few (and fuck you, by the way), or more likely, you're simply bad at assessing the moods of the people you work with. Out of touch, in other words. Statistics vary widely, but after crunching the numbers, what comes across clearly is that a significant percentage of U.S. wage earners are unhappy in the workplace. There's a host of reasons why this is so, and naturally the degree of dissatisfaction varies depending on a range of both personal and environmental factors. Now, tab your preferred psychographic snapshot and consider that most folks work at least eight hours a day. Where does that leave us? One third of most folks' lives down the tubes. That's where.

Let's see: we spend a third of our lives sleeping (the little death), and another third on the clock. At best, we learn to tolerate our work lives; at worst, we despise every borrowed minute. Chip off another hour for the average commute, and that leaves us with seven hours in which to enjoy the remaining happy parts of our lives.

But I think we can whittle that down a bit more. Next on the list: relationships.

In the United States, approximately half of all marriages end in divorce. The trend lines may fluctuate with time and cultural shifts, but quibbling doesn't add up to much here. Divorce is generally unpleasant, and every filing signals real and often profound dissatisfaction. Mark the ledger.

Of course, a marriage that ends badly wasn't a bad marriage all the way through. Was it? Nah, I won't take it that far, even though it's not unusual for one or both of the parties of the dissolved partnership to utter those infamous last words (or shriek them, as the case may be), "I'm not sure I EVER loved you!"

Here's the way I see the general progression of most relationships:

1. In the beginning, you're quite happy with each other. Perhaps even blissfully so.

2. A little further in, you're mostly happy, and still quite satisfied.

3. You're relatively satisfied, and sometimes quite happy.

4. Your relationship is best illustrated by a line punctuating peaks (satisfaction) and valleys (dissatisfaction).

5. The peaks are becoming less pronounced, and appearing far less frequently.

6. The valleys are becoming canyons, with lots of erosion going on between them.

I'll stop there. It's pretty obvious where things are heading. Yes, the progression I've laid out is somewhat oversimplified. But anyone reading in good faith has to admit that my little enumeration is sorta the way things are. At least, a lot of the time. This stuff isn't really complicated.

Now go fetch the guy floundering at relationship level #6 (I'll speak from a man's perspective, for obvious reasons), and take him out for lunch. How do you think it will go? Will we get a blow-by-blow account of his marital woes communicated around mouthfuls of moderately priced sub sandwich hold the mustard? Or are we more likely to spend the lunch hour small-talking the big game? Most likely it'll be the latter. Oh, and let's not write off our friend's selective silence as just another case of misplaced, testosterone-based male stoicism. That might be the shrimp cocktail, but there's a lot more brewing inside the shell of this steamed clam.

I spent the last five years of my marriage sleeping in a recliner chair in the living room. But up until the last year or so, I would have told you my marriage was relatively happy (that's the shrimp cocktail part talking). Furthermore, I would have insisted that I still loved my wife, and I would have meant it (clam part, and I'll pursue that ridiculous metaphor no further, I promise!). Of course, that was all a load of shit. I was miserable, and suicidal. At least I fantasized about suicide a lot. Knowing what my self-destruction would have done to my children, I kept the shotgun shells securely stowed away in the garage. I sat and stewed, always feeling like there was a car parked on top of my chest.

That is, until I finally let loose to my boss, who was also my best friend at the time. We'd grown up together. We knew each other better than our wives knew us. We were having lunch, actually—in a hospital cafeteria adjacent to a medical building we'd contracted to paint. We were probably involved in one of those inane conversations that most people have most of the time, but the next thing I knew I was venting like the God of the East Wind at a Norse confessional. I must have gone on for two hours about my conjugal miseries, while he just sat there, dumbfounded. Later that day, my friend admitted that he'd had absolutely no clue as to what was going on with me.

The next day we met for lunch again. The incident was replayed; this time in reverse. My friend filled me in on all the data points of his ill-being, things I'd never even guessed at. His marriage, his work, his goals. His whole fucking life. Most interesting was when he told me he *never realized he felt that way* until I confessed my troubles to him. We spent the next two or three weeks taking long lunch hours, commiserating. Sometimes raging, sometimes laughing. The laughter seemed to emerge from somewhere high up in the throat, like we were choking up something slightly rancid.

Had we really been hiding this shit all the time, even from ourselves? A little from column A, a little from column B, I suspect. A mixture of posturing, game-facing (because what else the hell are you gonna do?), and cool self-deception. It turns out that lying—to others, to ourselves—is a pretty kick-ass defense mechanism. And evolution, being concerned foremost with survival, has honed that puppy to a degree that we often fail to recognize.

So the next time somebody tells you they're glad to be alive, consider that what they likely mean to say is that they are generally happy, and then reflect on the notion that human beings are mostly lying bags of bones.

Still insisting most people are generally happy? Consider terminally ill children, collection notices, parents with Alzheimer's, family pets that usually don't make it beyond 11 or 12 years, migraines, fears of going to hell for having picked the wrong religion, blindness and limb removal (thanks to our good friend diabetes), prostate cancer, job loss (ain't that ironic, seeing as many of us hate our jobs?), sour milk, severe gastrointestinal and urinary disorders, bad teeth, unrequited love, quashed hopes, severed dreams, and death as the reward for all, good and bad alike.

Or just look at the faces. Listen to the stories when the masks come off. Who are you trying to convince?

If life is really so bad, isn't the solution staring you in the face? Why not kill yourself?

It's true that suicide is one logical option for ridding oneself of the pain of existence. It's the successfully chosen route for around a million people a year worldwide, while 20 to 30 times that number actually attempt it, but fail. Those aren't exactly inconsequential stats, by the way, considering the social stigma surrounding suicide, as well as the extreme psychological hurdles one must jump in order to do violent harm to one's own person. But there's a bigger picture to be seen here.

At risk of appearing prideful, I need to point out that philanthropic antinatalism emerges from a deep well of empathic sensibility, from which naturally springs a sense of responsibility toward other people, as well as toward all life. This isn't traditional sainthood I'm talking about. Believe me, I can play the self-righteous asshole when provided the proper arena. The point is that part, if not most, of what informs the antinatalist mindset is a certain kind of clarity that cuts through vast thickets of social conditioning to the taproot of our true, existential dilemma.

Life is suffering. The antinatalist wants first and foremost to cut suffering off at the root, through encouraging non-procreation. But in the end, he's just another person living among many. His life, like yours, is tied to the lives of his neighbors and loved ones—and especially to the lives of his own children. There is love, and indeed, a sense of duty. Yes, life is suffering, but part of that suffering is loss, especially loss through the death of a parent, or another beloved person.

But all of this is pretty fucking obvious, is it not? Finding Daddy hanging by the neck from the garage rafters isn't a good thing.

The only difference is that the antinatalist knows such a thing could have been prevented, if only Daddy had never been born.

> *Isn't the philosophy of antinatalism a dead-end approach to the world's problems? After all, the urge to procreate is biologically hard-wired, isn't it? Moreover, propagation of the species is culturally nurtured and supported in a thousand ways. Won't there always be more of them than there are of you?*

If antinatalism is a dead-end approach to the world's problems, pronatalism is a guarantor of their continuance. No people, no problems. As far as the urge to procreate is concerned, I'd contend that what you're really referring to here is the urge to fuck. Thanks to the 20th century development of pliable rubber, not to mention magical pills and creams and surgical snips (and in a pinch, the old but not-so-reliable "Pull out, you bastard!"), we can copulate at our leisure, retaining only the casual sideways glance toward wannabe Gramma's hatpin.

Ah, you say, but that's only the beginning of the story. There's also:

> A. The need for Mom to nurture;
> B. The need for Dad to feel like a 'real man' ("Hey, honey; why's he got the mailman's eyes?");
> B. The Feeling of Familial Fulfillment (the triple 'F');
> C. The need for future taxpayers;
> D. The need for soldiers to protect us (the 'children as cannon fodder' argument);
> E. The need to keep up the numbers, lest we be outbred and overrun by those other guys (the 'children as CULTURAL cannon fodder' argument);
> F. The need to be taken care of when we're old and worn out;

G. The need for the species to continue (vicarious immortality).

Notice a theme here? All these reasons are contrived to serve the begetter, and none the begotten. There IS that notion of granting the 'gift' of life to...to...uh, who was it receiving that gift, again?

Couldn't be the yet-to-be-conceived child, could it? What kind of present do you buy for a nonexistent non-entity who has nothing—not even the capacity to read the card, understand the sentiment, or unwrap the box? No, child creation and rearing is solely for those who will ultimately *benefit* from that child's presence. Be they parents, the larger society, organ donees, or the masters of Phlabius Fattus IV who are scheduled to arrive sometime in the year 2024 to abduct all labor-ready humans and ship them off to the inter-planetary zinc mines.

Of course, we don't dare tell them that. Instead we hold their unsolicited existence over their heads, eventually selling off their pieces into various avenues of servitude. "You owe us!" "You owe society!" "You owe God!" And if they're unhappy with the arrangement, tough shit. "You're stuck here now, buddy-boy. Quit being a baby and make the best of it!" Into the grinder, onto the assembly line, packed to ship, instructions included. Soldiers of the future, in a war where everybody eventually makes it to the front line, and stays there until they see that body bag with their name on it.

As far as there always being more of them (pronatalists) than there are of us (antinatalists): well, you've got a point there. Honestly, I can't envision my philosophy sweeping the planet anytime soon. Although there are a couple of points in my favor. For one thing, in those societies that are becoming increasingly secular and in other ways modern, the tendency to breed is downward. Call it materialistic selfishness. Call it lack of traditional values. Hell, call it the awareness that my view is the right view! Whatever, it's a good trend from my POV. Moreover, and lest we forget, any and every procreational temptation thwarted is a win for our side. A small victory, perhaps. Then again, if a group of skaters breaks through the ice and I manage to rescue only one or two, I've accomplished something, haven't I?

Then there are environmental factors. The fact that we are all part of a finite ecosystem is incontrovertible. There are limits to growth within a closed system, and no whining about 'the rights to my own body' or 'God's law' is going to change that. Unless we somehow manage to transform ourselves into electrical impulses in short order (ah, them lovable, wacky future-geeks), the shit is gonna come down. People are going to start dying in droves—not in the usual course that we are habituated to rationalize, but in dense concentrations that might actually make folks sit up and notice. For some reason, it seldom dawns on parents that they've delivered a death sentence upon their children's downy-soft little noggins, but the jolt of ubiquitous screaming headlines will get their attention: PEOPLE ARE DYING! ALL OVER THE FUCKING PLACE! MORE TO THIS STORY IN THE EVENING EDITION. (*Meanwhile, our alien lords on Phlabius Fattus IV have taken command...story continues on E-8*).

Anyhow, I've come up with some alternatives to the list of inducements above:

A. Get a doll, or maybe a puppy (be sure to adopt).
B. Do some push-ups, and lose the beer belly.
C. The less people, the less cost. Eventually, it'll all even out at zero. (Anyway, after death...no taxes!)
D. Fight your own goddamned wars.
E. Racial supremacy is so passé, and cultural supremacy will be meaningless after the people are gone.
F. Suck it up.

It can't be overstated. Vicarious immortality is NOT *real* immortality. When you're dead, you're dead. When you die, the world ends. When you die, civilization ends. The idea that you continue to survive through your children, or your country, or through the human race in general is patently absurd. It's an abstraction, people; a poetic metaphor invented to assuage your fear of mortality. Don't fall for it. You are going to die, and there'll be nothing left of you. I'm truly sorry that that's the way it is. It wasn't my idea, and there isn't anything anybody can do about it. Live your life, try and have some fun, but pay attention to all the times you're not having fun, and ask yourself: "Is this the stuff I want to foist on my future kids?" If you make yourself just slightly more aware of the situation than I was when I chose to breed, the answer will be crystal clear.

Isn't antinatalism the coward's way out? Part of what makes life so ultimately rewarding is facing challenges square on, and overcoming them. Remember the guy in that episode of The Twilight Zone *who died, and wound up in a place where he got everything he wanted? Turns out he was in Hell! If things are too easy, it all gets boring really fast, doesn't it?*

I get this one a lot.

I happen to agree that happiness is all wound up in the whole experiential human package. But when we talk about result-oriented, affirmative suffering—you know, 'pain makes gain,' 'you gotta climb that mountain to make it over to the shore' sort of motivational-speak—we can't just glibly overlook the fact that a lot of suffering has no purpose, leads to no victories, and in fact offers only a basically miserable existence for the sufferer. Why do you think the main emphasis in humanitarian work is to alleviate suffering? It's one thing to learn useful lessons from Miss Pain the austere schoolmistress, quite another to be constantly beaten over the ass with her barbed wire ruler during summer intermission (unless you're into that kind of thing).

The claim that antinatalism is "the coward's way out" is plain silly. What the hell is so courageous about being a breeder? "Look at me, I unloaded my nuts into somebody! Bring on the ticker-tape parade!" Oh, and there's the little fact that you're being 'brave' at somebody else's expense. Yeah, that. Look around you, Prince Valiant. The landscape is thick with guys swinging swords, townsmen and bumpkins alike, and gravid Guineveres are a dime per gross.

You really want to be a hero, Hero? Shrug off the conditioning and peer pressure, and consider that the life you DON'T bring into the world is the life that never gets eaten by the dragon.

Who says suffering is bad, anyway? You? Well, that's your opinion, but not everybody sees it like you do.

Who says suffering is bad? You do. Everybody does. Oh, it's one thing to consider pain, misery and affliction in the abstract, contextualized against a backdrop of fantasized hope-fors, or an escapist future utopia where all past hurts fade into utter forgetfulness. But nobody sits on a tack on purpose. Suffering is by definition that which we don't want to experience. Even if in those cases where we see it as a necessary obstacle to be overcome, eventually we want to *overcome* it? Don't we?

Must I repeat myself? Suffering isn't bad because God—or Plato, or Kant, or Superman—says it is; suffering is bad *because we don't like it*. We don't want it inflicted on us, or on the ones we care about.

Unfortunately, the choice to have children carries with it the de facto choice for our children, who have no say in the matter, to suffer, and die. We know it'll happen going in, yet we do it anyway, because we're selfish, and our selfishness creates a blind spot formed from a mixture of faith and ignorance behind which we hide our conscience. Of course, there are those others who just randomly propagate, and damn the consequences. I assume they won't be reading this book.

What gives you the right to make judgments as to who should and should not have kids? Who made you God?

God isn't here, and I am.

Aren't you being thoroughly hypocritical in asking others to forbear having children, seeing that you've already sired two of your own?

Yes, and former crack whores have no right to counsel presently active crack whores on the ill-advisability of crack-whoredom. The funny thing about mistakes is, you usually learn from them *after* you've made them.

I'm aware that my use of a descriptor like "mistake" to describe my two daughters might upset people. I'm not actually doing that, but I thought I'd confirm the emotional space most folks instantly jump to when this subject comes up. The truth is, it was my mistake all along. Unfortunately, my children will bear the brunt of my actions up until the day they die. Not always, and hopefully never too severely, although...who knows?

Do you think the parents of Steven Hicks, Steven Tuomi, James Doxtator, Richard Guerrero, Anthony Sears, Raymond Smith, Eddie Smith, Ernest Miller, David Thomas, Curtis Straughter, Errol Linsey, Tony Hughes, Konerak Sinthasomphone, Matt Turner, Jeremiah Weinberger, Oliver Lacy, and Joseph Bradehoft had any idea that their respective prides and joys would one day cross paths with a man named Jeffrey Dahmer? Did you even recognize any of the names?

Let's run down the list:

Steven Hicks. Strangled and dismembered, later smashed into pulp with a sledgehammer and sprinkled about the landscape.

Steven Tuomi. Murdered, dismembered, eventually thrown out with the garbage. No remains were ever found.

James Doxtator. Strangled, flesh removed with acid. Bones pulverized and disposed of.

Richard Guerrero. Strangled and dismembered.

Anthony Sears. Strangled, dismembered, head and genitals kept as trophies.

Raymond Smith. Strangled, corpse-raped, dismembered. His bones were placed around the apartment as ornaments.

Eddie Smith. Strangled, dismembered, dissolved with acid.

Ernest Miller. Throat cut, flesh removed, eaten.

David Thomas. Throat cut, flesh removed, eaten.

Curtis Straughter. Strangled, dismembered, dumped.

Errol Linsey. Strangled, corpse-raped, dismembered.

Tony Hughes. Strangled, dismembered, dissolved in acid after the corpse was left lying around the house for a couple days.

Konerak Sinthasomphone. While he was still alive, a hole was drilled into the back of his head and hydrochloric acid was injected into his brain, in an attempt to create a 'zombie.' He was eventually dismembered. Konerak was 14 years old.

Matt Turner. Strangled, dismembered.

Jeremiah Weinberger. Strangled, dismembered.

Oliver Lacy. Strangled, dismembered, corpse-raped, heart stored in refrigerator.

Joseph Bradehoft. Strangled, partly dismembered with head and torso kept in apartment.

Sorry I had to do that, but not nearly as sorry as I am for the victims and their surviving loved ones. I'm also sorry for Jeffrey, and especially for his parents. Imagine for a moment that any of these children might be one of your own, their lives cut short under such circumstances. Think about it for a minute. Then consider that the chances of any child's dying like this are actually pretty good. Oh, not necessarily as the result of the kind of brutality that grabs headlines. But you must realize that the mechanisms involved in the natural decline and ultimate demise of the body can be as horribly painful as anything Dahmer ever inflicted on his victims. Worse still, the suffering can stretch across a relatively extended gap of time, against which Dahmer's heinous ministrations might realistically be deemed short and sweet, ghastly images notwithstanding.

I live most days with these hypothetical realities swirling around in my head. People tell me I should learn to deal with it. Put it in perspective, whatever the fuck that means. Yes, I've tried to raise them right, and teach them how to be careful. But how can my inadequate little life lessons protect my children from their inevitable doom? They can't. My children will suffer in life, perhaps excruciatingly so, and there's very little I can do about it. And they will die. I committed as monstrous an act as Jeffrey Dahmer ever did, only instead of actually having the balls to commit the atrocities myself, I delivered my daughters over to the monster all tied up in pretty bows with shining, hopeful smiles that Daddy knew what he was doing when he started this whole thing.

For life IS Jeffrey Dahmer. Life eventually dopes us, strangles us, tears the flesh from our bones, fucks our every orifice, drills into our minds, and ultimately eats us up and throws our remains out with the trash. I love my children with every fiber of my being. But I hate myself even more for ever bringing them into existence.

You say antinatalism is all about reducing suffering, but can't you see that the universal absence of children (not to mention the concomitant, prescient dread with respect to the consequent extinction of the human race) would produce an all-inclusive, sublunary distress amongst the remaining populace? Doesn't the prospect of what amounts to a universal holocaust through procreative attrition give you pause?

Give me pause? Not much, really. It comes down to this. Everybody suffers, and everybody dies. What changes when you eliminate the procreative factor? Human suffering and death end with the death of the last man or woman. Procreation is both the initiator and the sustainer of illness, oppression, starvation, war and death.

In the film *Children of Men*, we are confronted with the vision of a world where human reproduction has come to a standstill. Early on in the movie, the youngest person left on earth is murdered. Whether done intentionally or not, this is a striking metaphor demonstrating how much we invest in the idea of the species continuing after our deaths. Stripped of our abstract, vicarious, fake immortality, what is left to us? The murder of the young man represents mankind's suicide in the face of his mortality.

Earlier I gave a brief account of my daughter's pertinent observation regarding the impending death of a family pet. "If this is how it ends," she asked, "what's the point?" That's the existential dilemma for which there is no answer, other than one born out of unsupported, hopeful fantasy.

There's a scene near the end of the film, probably my favorite, where Clive Owen carries the newborn 'miracle child' (yes, yet another apocalyptic cop-out!) through a part of the city that's become a war zone, in the middle of a fierce battle. For a moment, all hostilities cease while the participants gaze in reverent awe at the newborn hope of humanity. The tacit armistice manages to hold for about two minutes, not quite long enough for the noncombatants to clear the shot. Then the killing and maiming commences like before. Like always.

At the very end of the film, after mother and child are delivered safely into the arms of a group dedicated to repopulating the world, after the fadeout, you hear the sound of children's laughter. Like I said, cop-out. Nobody has the balls to end the world. There's always the hope that NEXT TIME we'll get it right. Never the acknowledgment that we never do; that we can't. That's why the movie always ends at the bright spot. We'll never find out what happened to our miracle child. Was she sexually molested growing up? Where is she now? Is she depressed? Sadistic? Is she a crack whore sucking cocks for $10 a shot back behind the Wal-Mart? Did she contract an immune deficiency disease related to the virus that originally rendered 99.8 percent of all men infertile? Does she wish she'd never been born? Will she commit suicide? Will she be murdered?

Two things for certain. She will suffer to some extent, and she will die. And for her, it will be as if she never were. When she dies, from her point of view, the universe ends with her. She will not live on through her offspring, nor they through theirs, nor they through theirs, and all that will be left of anybody will be worm food. And even the worms will die.

However, we have the choice to end all suffering and all death in a single generation. Not through violence—though surely violence will occur as it always does—but by simply opting out of the procreative cycle. Universal holocaust? Please.

Like it or not, every one of us is already interred in a death camp, just waiting in line for our turn at the ovens. Problem is, we keep opening the gates and inviting the extended family to the picnic.

Our suffering is already ensured. Our mothers and fathers saw to that. But we have the marvelous, ever-present opportunity to END IT HERE.

Let's, shall we?

> *In the end, isn't all this really about your own depression, perhaps based upon your personal bad choices, bad luck and failures? Isn't the axiom 'misery loves company' more than applicable in the case of your efforts here? To put it another way, aren't you simply projecting your own suicidal ideation onto the world?*

Maybe. At least, some of it.

On the other hand, any of us could diagnose our motivations into oblivion, and it really wouldn't make any fucking difference. The arguments are still what they are. Attempting to mitigate them by disparaging the source is just a roundabout way of killing the messenger.

On the *other* other hand, there are studies demonstrating that depressed people may actually have a better handle on reality than your run-of-the-mill optimist.

On the *third* hand (running out of hands here), it just might be that depression is actually the result of seeing life for what it really is, perhaps accompanied by the inability to filter existence through the various layers of fantasy and illusion that seem to be the cultural norm.

Pick a hand. Then deal with my reasoning. I'm quite open to counterarguments. I look for them. If nothing else, they help me tweak the nuances and clarify my thinking. Bring it on. You may even convince me that I'm wrong. You won't convince that I'm wrong because I'm sad.

If you had the means, just how would you carry out your morbid vision? How far would you go to get the job done?

This isn't an easy question to answer. To be honest, I'm not so sure I'm qualified to offer practical suggestions as to how to bring on humankind's extinction. I've never had a strong interest in politics for the simple reason that, due to the complexity of the body politic, I'm never quite certain what the end result of any particular legislation might be. Sometimes actions evoke very strong counter-reactions, especially in regard to a widely and deeply cherished myth like pronatalism.

Regardless, we run the risk of getting ahead of ourselves. At this point in history, I'm just hoping to start what I hope will be a continuing dialogue concerning a very taboo subject. My antinatalist ambitions are quite modest. I want to say it's all about supplying information, but that's not quite right. It's more about getting people to think about life in a different way—jumping up and down, waving my arms in an attempt to distract them from their self-deceptions and wishful thinking. If I can provoke them to look away, even momentarily, and to stare life straight in the face, I've got a good shot at getting them—some of them—to consider a different point of view.

Still, I feel like I'm avoiding the question. Let's go in the other direction, then. Out to the furthest reaches of my own wish-thinking. If I were a brilliant (though mad, by most accounts) scientific genius with a knack for genetic wizardry, would I design and introduce a biological superweapon with which to render all males impotent and/or all females barren?

You can bet your sweet bippy I would! And without any hesitation whatsoever. I'm sure I'd go down in the few remaining history books as a monster dwarfing all previous monsters. But what do I care? As I hope I've made clear by now, all of us have a little monster in us. All of us inflict suffering on other life-forms, human and nonhuman alike. By nipping procreation in the bud, all I'd be doing is calling the monsters' ball to an end. Admittedly, my actions would initially amp up the suffering quotient within the species. But the spike would only be temporary, followed by a relatively quick, subsequent plunge as the numbers of potential sufferers dwindled toward zero. And finally, there would be peace in the valley. At least, as far as the human race is concerned.

Still. Seems like I've missed something. Ah! The rest of the animal kingdom! Well, odds are pretty good the earth will be impacted by a giant meteorite sooner or later. Or maybe a comet. Or, if it somehow remains miraculously unscathed on this celestial bumper-pool table, the sun will surely get the job done when its gravitational restraints are loosened due to its expenditure of mass in heating this little corner of the galaxy, and it balloons out to the reach of our present orbit. Of course, that'll be billions of years from now; which is a shame, as every year means the suffering (on some level) of literally trillions of lower life-forms.

We do what we can.

Is it possible that you're wrong? Could there indeed by a reason for life to persist on this planet beyond the blind, evolutionary drive? God, or the tao, or Omega Point... or something along those lines? Or is there really nothing to hope for outside the pages of this trivial tale, pressed in between the immovable, uncompromising bookends of eternal nothingness?

Whose reasons, and why should I go along with them? In the hypothetical space encompassing all possibilities, there may indeed be metaphysical realities of which I am unaware. Gods, or other sorts of archetypal originators. Trans-dimensional flesh factories mass-producing DNA fashions and accessories under duress of quotas sanctioned by the faceless middle management at Tao, Inc. (not to be confused with Taco Bell). Space aliens with a hankering to bio-engineer just for the hell of it.

So what? Why should I submit to the whims of mysterious, otherworldly puppeteers plotting through questionable means to achieve some unknown purpose? Furthermore, how can we know that such a purpose isn't fundamentally malevolent?

Of course, I hope I've made myself clear about what I believe concerning life's ultimate meaning. As far as I can see, there is none. We're born, we suffer and die in the grasp of blind, cruel chance. Not always purposefully cruel, but cruel nonetheless. The reason we invent 'Holy Purpose' is precisely because we are in need of straws to clutch. All of us are drowning in a sea of cosmic indifference, and deep down I believe most of us know it. Our attempts at transcendence are nothing more than pathetic Hail Mary passes, launched as the clock times out, in the hope of discovering a loophole where none exists. And because we're desperate, we'll either hang onto laughably outmoded anthropomorphic expressions engineered by our despair, or we'll latch onto new gurus who promise us existential escape pods born of this or that sham singularity. Krishna, Jesus or Buck Rogers. All their promises are so much chimera.

But let's consider for a moment that the utopia of our dreams is attainable. What about those cracked bones and that withered flesh wrought into the ascending steps to Nirvana? To hell with all those multitudes who went before, so long as somebody, some day, gets a taste of that sweet, sweet Ambrosial nectar? What a bizarre and needless sacrifice! Especially when the (at least) next best thing continuously plays upon the nonexistent sensory apparatus of those who never were, and at the expense of no one.

And who's to say that even Nirvana lasts forever? Heaven is always represented as a static fantasy, where nothing ever changes, and everything is just fine. But how do we know this is the case? If there's one truth about human nature which the universal mythologies warn us about, it's that people always manage to fuck up a good thing. Or maybe we'll be kickin' it up there in the celestial paradise for a while, only to be usurped by the gods of universe H-4, who are jealous of our digs and wield bigger lightning bolts! Who needs that shit?

Nonexistence, on the other hand, is a sure bet. By definition, the nonexistent neither suffer, nor want for anything. They reside in a state of what I like to call 'negative bliss.' It is a state of perfect contentment, where no desire goes unfulfilled because there's no desire to begin with.

This may seem like a bit of a word game, but think about it. Let's try to flesh out the difference between the two states, existence vs. nonexistence, for comparison. Imagine for a moment that you are in a relatively neutral existential state. Say, lying in bed, and staring at the ceiling. Suddenly the Devil appears at the foot of your bed, and makes you an offer:

"Hey there! You're looking a little bored, if I might be so bold. Tell you what. How's about I offer you the most remarkable hour of sex you've ever had? Or perhaps you'd prefer a sumptuous feast on a culinary scale hitherto unknown? Hell has the best chefs! Or are altered states of consciousness more to your liking? Our heroin is pure, our cocaine uncut, and our lab-tested hallucinogens are guaranteed to blow your mind on several levels. Any or all of this, on the condition that you also allow me to subject you to a round of the most dreadful, continuous physical and mental torture you can imagine. What do you say, champ? Want to give it a go?"

Male posturing aside, I can tell you what I'd choose, and what anybody would choose if they've ever experienced a great deal of severe physical pain or psychological turmoil. Admittedly, someone who's lived a rather charmed life up to this point might be tempted to take the bait—once. Never twice.

Now, you might argue that my example speaks to life's gross extremes, and doesn't fairly represent what living is like for most people, most of the time. Two points:

First, I'll acknowledge I've painted the problem in sharp, contrasting colors. The demarcations between pain and pleasure aren't usually quite so vivid in the real world. In fact, I'd go so far as to say that most experiences are a mixture of the two. That said, I must note (from personal experience) that pain usually arrives a bit less tainted by pleasure than the other way around. Yes, there are peaks of happiness where we seem to be truly lost in the moment, but these are rare. The much more common form of happiness seems to be a sort of hard-won equilibrium, a transient 'floating on top' of anxieties, easily tipped over by the next mini- or maxi-crisis (and our days are filled with such crises, though we tend to ferret a lot of that shit out of our memories in order to maintain our personal life-lies).

But. When we're *truly* suffering, there's seldom anything to smile about. While happiness may represent the sundeck on an ocean liner, suffering is the rudder that steers the ship. It's nice to get out on clear days, soak up some rays, maybe sneak in under the lifeboat's tarp and procure a little nookie. But navigation is mostly out of our hands (and for a hard determinist like me, it's *completely* out of our hands). Unplanned course changes are inevitable, as is foul weather. And lest we forget, every life-cruise—and I mean EVERY one—ends up like the Titanic.

Another point I want to make is that, while the extremes of happiness outlined in my examples are relatively rare, extremes of suffering are not so rare. There is still torture on this planet, both physical and psychological, rivaling that of the Inquisition (and I suspect ofttimes surpassing that, thanks to the gods of modern technology). Stroke, various forms of painful cancer, bone diseases, emphysema (drowning in your own body fluid), and a host of other grievous medical conditions await those of us 'fortunate' enough to have survived to a certain age and who aren't lucky enough to die suddenly in our sleep. Add to that the psychological suffering that drives tens of millions of us to attempt suicide every year, while several times that many drink and drug themselves into stupor.

We know our children will suffer in life. We also know they'll die. Knowing this, what is our moral justification for bringing them into existence (beyond the insipid 'God told me to' mantra of the faithful)? The only relatively altruistic one I can think of is the wish to bestow happiness upon someone we care for (note, I said "relatively" altruistic). This is a noble aim when we're talking about helping someone who already exists, perhaps by adopting a child. But the nonexistent don't need happiness. Nor do they have any desire for it. The nonexistent already dwell in a perfect place, a state of absolute peace and contentment; forever undisturbed by want, or fear, or tumult, or indeed by any change at all. This is the State of Negative Bliss (SNB); and unlike the Heaven of religious fantasy, the SNB is a very real place—in a negative sort of way, of course.

Many would argue that I'm misrepresenting the actual state of affairs here, and would indeed question the validity of referring to nonexistence as any kind of 'state' at all. In philosophy, this is part of what's referred to as the 'non-identity' problem. What it boils down to is that nonexistent entities aren't really entities at all, but presupposed abstractions. This being the case, concerns about their future welfare (including future harm) are misplaced, and inapplicable.

But does anybody really believe this? As a short, hypothetical test case, let's review something I wrote earlier, and suppose we live in a world where every child is tortured and killed shortly after birth. Can anybody reasonably argue that the obvious moral implications involving the choice to conceive in such a world would be invalid on account of 'non-identity'? That such a question can even be asked with a straight face goes to show what happens when moral philosophy drifts too far away from its groundings in human sensibility. It's obvious (to me, anyway) that morality encompasses questions regarding future states, which automatically comprise the transition from the potential to the actual. Whether we're talking about the potential conditions regarding existing people or potential people makes little difference to me.

As it happens, I consider the SNB to be a very real state. Nonexistence, as far as personhood is concerned, may not have many definable attributes, but it has one. It is the default state of life, and of consciousness. Nonexistence stretches out eternally behind us, as well as in front of us. This existence is, indeed, a trivial tale pressed between the bookends of eternal nothingness. But within that eternal nothingness lies the kingdom of the SNB. The SNB was our original home, until we were yanked out by life's self-replicating compulsion into this world of promise and loss. All of us will return to the SNB in due time, bearing no memories of our sojourn here.

At least, I hope so.

Alternatively, the theistic heaven promises an eternity of torture for nonbelief. And the Eastern esotericas hint at endless cycles of reincarnation, from Godhood to amoeba and back again. I'm not sure which is worse, but I know it would have been far better had I never been brought into an existence where either is even hypothetically possible.

What's life done to you, to embitter you this way?

What? Did you start at the end of the book?

Epilogue

I grew up in a typical middle-class neighborhood. You know—one- and two-story tract houses, kids on bikes, the occasional adultery and wife beating. That sort of thing.

When I was eight or nine, I guess, this guy moved in across the street from us. I don't know where he worked or where he lived before. He just showed up one day and soon it was like he'd always been there. He seemed nice enough. And not having a family of his own, he sort of latched onto us neighborhood kids. He let us skate and play football out in the street in front of his house. Sometimes he would even join in. When it was hot, he'd make a big pitcher of Kool-Aid and bring it out to us at the end of our games.

And, oh man, the barbecues! Every evening out in his driveway, he'd be there turning the meat. Anybody in the neighborhood was welcome to drop by and sample whatever he had on the fire. His cooking wasn't always the greatest; sort of hit-and-miss, I guess. But he always had cookies and soda pop, which kept me and my friends dropping by night after night.

I don't mean to say the guy was some sort of a saint. He could be surly at times. And his moods were unpredictable, at least to a kid. There were times—not many, but more than a few—when he would become impatient with us, and things would get rough. The first time he hit one of my friends, I ran home to tell my parents what had happened, but they didn't seem too concerned. My dad just muttered something about how the kid probably learned a lesson, and mom kept quiet. Seems that most of us met the guy's backhand sooner or later. Every time it happened, we'd get pissy and run crying to our rooms, cursing into our wet pillows. But most of us got over it pretty fast, and before long we'd be back out on the guy's front lawn, tossing the frisbee and listening to his dirty jokes and war stories. Most of us loved the guy.

Our parents' attitude toward him was a bit different, though my dad seemed to like the guy. They watched football together on the weekends, sucking down Schlitzes and laughing their asses off in the living room. But once in a while things would go off track. I barely recall some things being said about my dad's work or something, and before you knew it they were out in the backyard trading punches. I'd always thought my dad was pretty tough, but this guy wasted him and walked away without a scratch.

I guess my dad eventually managed to dust himself off and put on his old game face. He grumbled more than before, usually about "the state of the neighborhood," but you could see that he'd been stung hard. Even if he never mentioned it. I think the guy wound up apologizing to my dad. At least I remember seeing them shake hands. After that, everything went back to normal; though I did notice that my dad developed an almost imperceptible flinch whenever the guy was around.

Mom was a different story. When the guy first moved in, she steered the welcoming committee. I remember standing by her side as she rang the bell at his doorstep, bearing a pot roast that she'd spent most of the day preparing. "Welcome to our neighborhood!" she said as she handed him the roast. The guy was gracious and we all smiled and they exchanged niceties that I didn't quite understand. Mom showed up for most of the barbecues, too. She even pitched in with the cleanup afterward, which always seemed strange to me since I knew how she hated getting her hands dirty. Thinking back now, I wonder if they didn't have a brief affair. But then my dad was always around, smiling and joining in, so probably not. Come to think of it, I believe the guy was even invited to a couple of my little brothers' christenings. More likely, I think she was just taken in by the guy's charm. Maybe she was a little infatuated. Like most of us were. Initially.

But there were times when I came home from school and I'd catch my mom sitting in the front alcove, peeking out through the sheers across the street. I can still remember that look on her face. I never was sure if it was fear, or maybe dread. What was really weird, though, was that it was always accompanied by a tight little smile. Forced looking, like she didn't really want to believe what she was thinking.

Life went on. Business as usual in the burbs. Until that kid Martin disappeared. He lived up on the corner, nearest to the main street. He was maybe a year younger than I. He used to hang over at the guy's house quite a bit, playing frisbee and shit. I remember him being a really fast runner for his age. What happened was, I was out fucking around after school one afternoon, and I noticed his parents and a big group of neighbors in the driveway. Most of them were crying.

I looked across the street, and there was the guy, sitting in his lawn chair and looking in their direction. Drinking a beer. He watched for a while, then he got up and went back into the house, leaving that ratty old chair on the lawn.

Martin never did turn up. Just one of those mysteries.

Martin's folks moved away shortly after that. Everything eventually went back to normal, though all the parents were a little more cautious for awhile. Made us hold our little brothers' and sisters' hands when crossing the street. The buddy system, or something.

My mom took to looking out the window more frequently, still with that look on her face. Dad found a new job.

Life went on. Years went by.

I somehow shoehorned my way into high school. I was never what you would call a conscientious student, but I graduated and got a job at the liquor store down the street. My folks' marriage followed the downhill slope, and eventually they split up.

Did I mention a couple more kids disappeared? Just a couple more, I think. Come to think of it several adults disappeared within that span of years as well. Of course, it makes more of an impact when it's a kid. So much to look forward to, life cut short, and all that bullshit. Each disappearance signaled a little interruption in the order of things, but you know what they say about getting back up on that bike. My neighborhood had a lot of bikes.

I went back to the old neighborhood recently. I didn't see anybody I recognized. All new faces, most of them from south of the border. Except…that guy! He was still there, sitting in what I swear was the same old lawn chair out in his driveway. It didn't seem that he had aged at all. He'd gotten a new barbecue, one of those propane ones with the burners like on a regular stove. I could smell the smoke coming out of it, only it didn't smell nearly as good as when I was a kid. A bit overdone, perhaps.

It was the weekend, and a lot of people were out in the street, passing by, some stopping to chat, or to sample what was on offer. I thought I saw one or two purposely cross to the other side of the street, but that could've been my imagination. More likely, the smoke was getting to me.

The guy looked up and saw me, idling in my car by the curb. I saw a glint of instant recognition light up his face, and he extended his right arm stiffly up in greeting. I looked down like I was checking a map or something, then I drove slowly away. But I could feel the guy's eyes on the back of my neck, even after I went around the corner.

...Of Skating

The thin ice cracks.
The skater screams.
The struggles cease.
The hole freezes over.
The village dreams...

Acknowledgements

Thanks to my friend and publisher, Chip Smith, without whom this work of love and hate would never have been conceived, much less actually finished. Thanks also to Cia (she knows why), and to TGGP and Ann Sterzinger for their much-needed proofreading skills. And lastly, I want to thank my mother, Judy—because I love her in spite of her procreative efforts, but most of all, because she insists. Oh, and let me not forget the many dogs, cats, rats, birds and fish I've loved and lost, who have taught me empathy, and how to be a bad loser.

JIM CRAWFORD is a short-order cook and part-time poet who lives in Riverside, California. Jim's online writing is archived at antinatalism.net. This is his first book.

ninebandedbooks.com

Made in the USA
Middletown, DE
02 April 2019